Inside the Literacy Hour

Learning from classroom experience

Ros Fisher

London and New York

First published 2002
by RoutledgeFalmer
11 New Fetter Lane, London EC4P 4EE

Simultaneously published in the USA and Canada
by RoutledgeFalmer
29 West 35th Street, New York, NY 10001

RoutledgeFalmer is an imprint of the Taylor & Francis Group

© 2002 Ros Fisher

Typeset in Sabon by Exe Valley Dataset Ltd, Exeter
Printed and bound in Malta by
Gutenberg Press Ltd

British Library Cataloging in Publication Data
A catalogue record for this book is available
from the British Library

Library of Congress Cataloging in Publication Data

Fisher, Ros
 Inside the literacy hour: learning from classroom experience/Ros Fisher
  p. cm.
 Includes bibliographical references and index.
 ISBN 0–415–25672–0 ISBN 0–415–25673–9 (pbk)
 1. Language arts (Elementary)–Great Britain. I. Title.

LB1576.F453 2002
372.6'0941–dc21   2001052023

ISBN 0–415–25672–0 (hbk)
ISBN 0–415–25673–9 (pbk)

Contents

List of tables   vii
List of figures   viii
Acknowledgements   ix

Introduction   1

1   Improving the teaching of literacy   3

2   The research project   20

3   Inside the literacy hour classroom   33

4   Learning to read in the literacy hour   50

5   Learning to write in the literacy hour   68

6   Changing practice at Key Stage 1   85

7   The literacy hour at Key Stage 2   100

8   The literacy hour in mixed-age classes   118

9   Four-year-olds and the literacy hour   134

10   Teachers and the literacy hour   151

11   Implications for research, policy and practice   166

Appendices   174

I   Interview schedules at the start and end of the year   174
II   Observation schedule for literacy hour   178
III Observation schedule for target children   180
IV   Questionnaire and interview schedule at end of the second year   181
V   Ethics protocol   182

References   183
Index   189

Tables

3.1 Observed use of the literacy hour in research classrooms   35

4.1 National Test Results for English at Key Stage 1 and 2, 1996–2000   50

4.2 Results of the October and June tests for each class   53

4.3 Statistics for reading test scores   55

4.4 Progress scores for each class   56

4.5 Analysis of variance between classes   57

4.6 Distribution of poor, average and good progress according to gender of children in the class   58

4.7 Distribution of poor, average and good progress according to number of children in the class   58

4.8 Distribution of poor, average and good progress according to number of year groups in the class   59

4.9 Distribution of poor, average and good progress according to age position in the class   60

4.10 Distribution of poor, average and good progress according to child's score in October   61

5.1 Distribution of good and little progress in writing according to who did guided writing   73

7.1 Key Stage 2 English test scores for Yew Tree Primary School   103

8.1 Teachers' views of the literacy hour in small schools in 1998 and 2000   122

10.1 Percentage of positive and negative views about the literacy hour in 1998 and 2000   161

Figures

1.1 Balance of teacher input and pupil effort   14
2.1 Programme of data collection   24
3.1 Use of objectives   40
5.1 Rachel, aged 10 years, showing influence of writing frame   78
5.2 Rachel, aged 10 years, *The Final Chapter*   80
7.1 Extract from Lana's (year 6) writing in September 1998   104
7.2 Extract from Lana's (year 6) writing in June 1999   104
8.1 Key points for mixed-age classes   124
9.1 Examples of differences in approach to involvement of
     4-year-olds in the literacy hour   137–8
9.2 Annie's writing in September   148
9.3 Annie's writing in July   148

Acknowledgements

This book would not have been written without the generous support and co-operation of the schools, teachers and children whose work is described here. They allowed us into their classrooms to watch them teach and talked freely to us about their work at a time when they were under great pressure to teach in a way that, for many, seemed quite different to what they had done before.

The research, an investigation into the implementation of a literacy hour in small rural schools (R000222608), was funded by the Economic and Social Research Council from September 1998 until January 2000. The University of Plymouth funded the follow-up study in June 2000. I am particularly grateful to my co-director on the project, Maureen Lewis, for her help in the design and analysis of the research. Bernie Davis, the research assistant on the project, conducted most of the interviews and collected all of the observational data. Her careful observation and sensitive writing of field notes has made it possible to illustrate the findings of the research as I have done in this book. I am grateful to her for this and for her collaboration on the chapter about 4-year-olds.

ROS FISHER
May 2001

Introduction

The National Literacy Strategy (NLS) was introduced into most primary (4–11) schools in England in September 1998. This book follows the thoughts and teaching of a group of teachers over the first two years of the strategy. The data were collected in the first year as an Economic and Social Research Council-funded research project that studied the implementation of the literacy hour in small rural schools. Twenty teachers were observed teaching an hour of literacy each month in the first year of the NLS; they were interviewed at the beginning and end of this year; children in their classes were given a reading test at the beginning and end of the year and writing samples were collected from target children in each class. At the end of the second year, twelve of these teachers were interviewed again and a further literacy hour was observed.

The research did not set out to identify successful teachers from this small sample. Our intentions were to give a detailed picture of what individual teachers were doing in the classroom during this time of imposed changes in the teaching of literacy. The test data and writing samples provided some indication of progress in each class and were used to support (or challenge) the judgements of the research team. The research does not provide answers to questions about the best way to teach reading and writing but it does provide some insights into what teachers were trying to do and how they went about it. Although there are no definitive answers, I try to draw out from our observations and what teachers themselves said, advice for others who are teaching reading and writing to primary age children.

The first chapter reviews some of the recent literature about the effective teaching of literacy and raises some questions about the feasibility of changing the way teachers teach through a large-scale project such as the NLS. The second chapter describes and evaluates the research itself, giving details of the design, methods, data collection and analysis. Questions about reliability, validity and ethical considerations are discussed. In Chapter 3, the way the teachers in our study went about introducing the literacy hour and how they integrated features of the NLS into their teaching is described. Certain aspects of the literacy hour were welcomed and implemented quickly. Others appeared more difficult to manage and were introduced more slowly. Whereas some teachers made changes to the way they taught, others did little more than change the timing of their lessons. Some readers may prefer to start with this chapter rather than with the two more theoretical opening chapters.

Chapters 4 and 5 consider how reading and writing is taught in the NLS. The findings from this research support other evidence that shows the impact of changes to the teaching of reading since the implementation of the NLS. Findings also indicate that the teaching of writing was slower to change. Chapter 4 describes how teachers in this study went about teaching reading in the literacy hour and Chapter 5 focuses on writing. The impact this teaching may have had on children's progress is examined. Each chapter ends with some advice for teachers about teaching reading and writing in the literacy hour.

How one successful Key Stage 1 teacher went about implementing the literacy hour in its first year is discussed in Chapter 6. What she said and how she taught is described showing that over the two years there were considerable changes to the way she planned and taught literacy. Chapter 7 takes an experienced Key Stage 2 teacher who was already teaching in many ways like the model proposed by the NLS. What she did and how she modified the hour are explained. Chapter 8 explores the way these teachers, all of whom worked in mixed-age classes, managed the planning and teaching of the NLS with its teaching objectives designed for specific year groups. Each of these chapters also ends with advice about how teachers might address the particular challenges that faced these teachers.

Chapter 9 considers the literacy hour with the youngest children in school. For this chapter I am indebted to Bernie Davis, our research assistant on the project. In addition to her work as research assistant, she studied the 4-year-olds specifically for her own doctoral research. She has gone through the project data and her own records to co-author this chapter. In it we argue that the quality of provision for 4-year-olds is particularly important at this sensitive time in their education. From what our teachers said and our observations of four-year-olds in the literacy hour, we offer advice for teachers of the youngest children, whether in mixed- or single-age classes.

Chapter 10 considers evidence from the ESRC-funded project and a questionnaire survey undertaken at the beginning of the NLS and after two years. It examines how teachers' ideas about literacy teaching have changed. What teachers said and evidence from classroom observations after two years of the NLS point to the possibility that evidence of change in teaching style may be more in the minds of teachers than in reality. Chapter 11 summarises the findings and points to ways forward for teachers, policy-makers and researchers.

The National Literacy Strategy is being evaluated by large-scale, government-sponsored research, both internally by the Office for Standards in Education (Ofsted) and externally by an international team from the University of Ontario under Michael Fullan. It is also important that small-scale in-depth studies are available to give voice to the teachers themselves and provide a fuller picture of what actually happened in classrooms.

1 Improving the teaching of literacy

Introduction

The quest to raise standards of literacy is long-standing and widespread. Throughout the twentieth century and into the twenty-first, if not before, educationalists have debated and experimented to discover the best way to teach children to read and write. The complexity of this endeavour is shown by the fact that the debates and the experiments continue. Recent initiatives world-wide have gone beyond previous attempts to describe methods (e.g. whole language versus phonic approaches) and now major teaching programmes have been introduced which adopt combinations of approaches in which both the content and the structure of the lesson is prescribed. The Early Years Literacy Programme in Victoria, Australia (DEET, 1997, 1998, 1999) involves a 2-hour teaching period with defined elements. Success for All (now called Roots and Wings) (Slavin, 1996) entails a 90-minute block of teaching and is currently used in many schools around the world. The NLS in England with only 1 hour of literacy teaching is now used in most English Primary (4–11) schools. All three claim large measures of success in raising literacy standards.

The NLS has aroused a good deal of interest around the world as a large-scale national initiative to raise standards of literacy. Initial results look promising, but test data conceal the detail. The research described in this book was undertaken over the first two years of the NLS in England. Twenty teachers were observed once a month teaching the literacy hour and interviewed twice in the first year. Twelve of these teachers were observed and interviewed again at the end of the second year. These data provide the opportunity to examine in depth what was happening in classrooms during the literacy hour.

In the first part of this chapter I want to consider where the renewed urgency to raise standards has come from and what kind of view of literacy this reflects. The raising of standards implies the measurement of those standards but herein lies a tension between the attainment of quantifiable outcomes and the recognition that there is more to being literate than that which can be measured. Within the opportunities offered by literacy lie attitudes and abilities that are not easily assessed. I want to recognise the difficulty of assessing literacy but acknowledge that, if we are to move forward in the search for improved teaching, we have to use all the means we can to judge efficacy. With this in mind, I want to examine the literature about the effective teaching of literacy. We can learn a lot from this but must not let it lure us into a simplistic view of teaching and learning. These are complex processes that involve an intricate interaction between teacher, learner and what is learned. I shall conclude the chapter by examining the model of teaching proposed by the NLS, drawing together ideas about teaching and learning and considering how the NLS attempts to combine these.

It is not my intention to provide a critique of the literacy strategy. This book offers evidence to contribute to its evaluation. Whether the NLS turns out to be a straightjacket or 'highly flexible framework' (Beard, 2002) time has yet to tell. Views of educationalists vary but it is teachers who have to work with it and who have to make sense of the rhetoric written about it. This chapter considers some of the background theory and evidence that influence current ideas about the teaching of literacy.

Raising literacy standards

> There has never before been a major national initiative to enable all primary teachers to learn the most effective methods of teaching literacy and how to apply them. . . . It will be the most ambitious attempt ever in this country to change for the better teaching approaches across the entire education service.
>
> (DfEE, 1997: paras 26/27)

This statement set the agenda for the introduction of the NLS in all English primary schools from September 1998. The NLS was based on the National Literacy Project (NLP) which had been introduced two years earlier in twenty-three local education authorities around England to raise standards in areas where results from national tests showed these to be lower than average. The NLS set the target that 'By 2002 80% of 11 year olds should reach the standard expected in English for their age (i.e. Level 4) in the Key Stage 2 National Curriculum tests' (ibid.: para. 1). Despite the fact that there was, at that time, no evaluation of the effectiveness of the NLP, the newly elected labour government decided to go ahead with full-scale implementation.

Looking carefully at the statement above, we can see that there are several implied values lying behind what was said. In particular, these suggest that there is a need to raise literacy standards and that the way to do this is by improving teaching. Furthermore, in the rhetoric associated with the launch of the Literacy Strategy, the setting of national targets whereby to measure the ensuing improvement clearly defined the parameters of literacy and what is seen as improvement in literacy. The setting of these targets implies a view of literacy as something that can be measured by end of year tests. It is clearly not as simple as this, success or failure of this initiative to develop an effective pedagogy will only be evidenced by the adults of the future – how effectively they can use literacy for their own purposes and with how much satisfaction they pursue their own literacy interests.

Standards of literacy, today even more than in the past, represent a high status, high stakes issue. The literacy demands on adults in the electronic age become ever more challenging and governments increasingly link high standards of literacy with economic growth. In a recent report on the education sector, the World Bank (1999) asserted education to be one of the best investments as return from education expenditure outstrips many investments in physical capital.

In Great Britain, the General Household Survey for 1995 showed that university graduates were likely to have higher salaries and were less likely to be unemployed. The report concludes that 'those with the greatest income were those with the highest literacy skills. . . . People at the lowest levels of literacy were more likely to be on a low income' (Office of National Statistics, 1996). There can be no doubt that the need for individuals to achieve high standards of literacy is increasing. And this is not only an economic imperative on a national scale but also an individual exigency at a very personal level. Literacy is one of the key tools for success in today's world and also an unparalleled means of recreation and personal discovery.

Evidence of the need to raise standards

There is general agreement that some youngsters leave secondary school with insufficient standards of literacy to enable them to lead a full life, but this is where the agreement ends. The extent and nature of the problem is a topic of continuing controversy. Listed below are some of the views that are expressed as part of this debate.

- Standards of literacy have fallen over the last 50 years.
- Although the highest achieving children in school in the UK are as good as children anywhere else in the world, there are more children here who do not reach an acceptable standard than there are in other developed countries.
- The demands of literacy have increased in recent years making previous standards inadequate.
- In order to raise standards we need to reform schools and teaching methods.
- The existence of such a large number of underachievers owes far more to poor standards of living than to poor teaching.

The opening chapter of a book that is essentially an analysis of practice is not the place to review in detail each of the preceding propositions. In brief, although there is no universal agreement on the opinions outlined here, there is some compelling evidence. Brooks (1998) reviewed the trends in the literacy of school children in the UK from national surveys undertaken between 1948 and 1996. He concludes:

> The major feature of the national results throughout UK is their great stability over time; most comparisons reveal no change, a few show a rise, even fewer show a fall. Fastening on isolated instances of a fall in average scores is to misrepresent the facts; and there is certainly no warrant for the repeated claims of decline – though there is always a case for improvement.
>
> (Brooks, 1998: 3)

[handwritten margin note: Good Quote]

This review also supports the proposition that, compared to other developed countries, there is a significant proportion of children who have poor literacy skills. This feature of international comparisons was noted as early as 1960 as well as in 1970 and again in 1996 (ibid., 1998).

Certainly, economic changes have resulted in literacy being an important skill in almost every employment context. Whereas there used to be a demand for many workers to staff production lines, now few jobs have no need for some use of literacy. In personal life, despite the concern that the electronic age will lessen the reading of books as recreation, the information explosion that has resulted from the World Wide Web and other aspects of the world today mean that everyone needs to be literate to get the most from their daily life. Thus the accessibility of information and written language in a range of forms means that literacy demands on every member of society have grown and it is increasingly difficult to thrive without a level of literacy that is at least adequate for life today.

If we recognise this growing need for a larger number of children to achieve their potential as literate adults, we must agree that we should look to how literacy is taught to raise standards even if it is not the standards that have fallen but the increased demands that give rise to this imperative. There is evidence that shows that low standards of literacy are associated with low standards of living (Gorman and Fernandez, 1992). Surely though, this is no reason for complacency but gives greater incentive to find ways of helping individuals overcome disadvantage by raising their achievement in literacy?

Thus I would argue that, although standards may not have fallen across the board, there is a need for increased levels of literacy for all children. In addition, although social disadvantage may make it more likely that children achieve lower standards, this does not have to be the case. There are schools and teachers who succeed, even against the odds, to help children develop as confident and effective readers and writers. There seems to be no real evidence that the teaching of literacy before the introduction of the NLS was poor but that it has been more effective in some schools and classes than others. We need to learn what we can from these teachers and these schools. Yet the question remains as to how possible it is to transfer effective practice from one context to another.

Effective schools/effective teachers

This concern to identify what it is that makes some schools or some teachers more effective than others is an alluring one. Indeed findings from school effectiveness studies in the 1980s and 1990s question the assumptions from the 1960s and 1970s that social background determines academic achievement. Research such as the Junior Schools Project (Mortimore *et al.*, 1988) showed school factors to be four times more important than factors such as gender or home background. Although home background is acknowledged to play an important part in children's subsequent achievement, schools can and do make a difference. Some have found that the impact is greater for primary schools than secondary schools (Sammons *et al.*, 1993) and for children with low attainment on starting school (Sammons *et al.*, 1995).

Scheerens (1992) in a meta-analysis of the international evidence from school effectiveness research identifies two widely accepted characteristics of school effectiveness:

- Structured teaching, which involves making learning objectives explicit, a well-planned sequence, regular testing and immediate feedback.
- Effective learning time which includes use of whole class teaching as this maximises the time pupils have with the teachers' attention, focus on a particular subject and the importance of challenge and praise.

Beard (1999) in a retrospective analysis of the principles underlying the NLS draws on evidence from both school effectiveness research and inspection reports. He argues that the importance afforded in the NLS to direct teaching, high-quality interaction and focused teaching are all supported by research in the UK and worldwide (Mortimore *et al.*, 1988; Scheerens, 1992; Reynolds, 1998). Indeed, the National Literacy Strategy Framework for Teaching itself asserts that the most successful teaching is discursive, interactive, well-paced, confident, ambitious (DfEE, 1998: 8). These features of successful teaching figure in many studies of teacher effectiveness.

Discursive and interactive are features mentioned by Brophy (1986) and Borich (1986) in the USA. In Britain, Mortimore *et al.* (1988) found that children performed better the more communication they had with their teacher about their work and where teachers used higher order questioning. The pace of lessons has also been found to be an important feature of

literacy teaching. Medwell *et al.* (1998) found that the lessons of
teachers of literacy were all conducted at a brisk pace with regular
ising of children's attention to the task at hand. Confident teaching,
in which teachers have a clear understanding of the objectives, relates to
the relatively new area of enquiry into the effect of teachers' subject
knowledge. Medwell *et al.*, considered the importance of subject knowledge for effective teachers and found that, whereas effective teachers did
not necessarily have an explicit knowledge base, they used their knowledge
implicitly in their teaching. In effect, these teachers' knowledge base was
their pedagogical content knowledge. Finally, ambitious teaching, where
teachers have high expectations of pupils, is generally agreed to be a factor
in successful teaching (Borich, 1986; Mortimore *et al.*, 1988; Ofsted, 1996).
Thus the description of teaching proposed by the NLS represents what
research into school and teacher effectiveness has shown to be associated
with effective practice.

However, interpretation of the words used to describe teaching can vary.
Questions have been raised about the nature of interactive teaching. Many
researchers (Galton *et al.*, 1980; Edwards and Mercer, 1987; Alexander,
1992) emphasise the understanding and skill that is needed to create high
quality interaction. Wells (1999) points out that 'high quality interaction'
means different things to different people. For those concerned with
'cultural reproduction' and the achievement of predefined goals it means a
style of discourse in which the teacher leads pupils in a triadic dialogue of
initiation, response and some sort of feedback. Although this can challenge
and extend thinking, it is ultimately a controlling strategy leading to predetermined outcomes. On the other hand, he argues that those who
criticise triadic discourse and consider high quality interaction to be a more
equitable process in which the teacher refrains from a litany of questions
and allows the child to adopt an initiating role are more concerned with
the empowerment of learners. Thus, reliance on findings from school effectiveness research promotes a particular model of teaching and learning,
which may be successful in achieving short-term gains but could be less
effective in developing lifelong attitudes and flexible literate behaviour.

In addition, Reynolds (1998) argues that, whilst the NLS reflects many
of the effectiveness factors identified by research, there is growing evidence
of 'context specificity' in the actual factors associated with learning gains
with different groups of children. In other words, different approaches may
be more appropriate in certain contexts than others. This gives rise to the
question as to whether the NLS, which presents the same model to all
teachers in all primary schools, can be uniformly effective in all contexts.
Alexander *et al.* (1995) point to a range of other features from the literature that are important in effective teaching. These can be summarised
under the heading: pedagogical flexibility. This includes features such as
the ability to provide a bridge between what the learner already knows and
what is taught (Vygotsky, 1962, 1978; Bruner and Haste, 1987). Also

important is the teacher's possession of a broad repertoire of organisational strategies and the ability to deploy these flexibly and appropriately (Gipps, 1992; Alexander, 1992).

Large-scale reform

It is one thing to identify features of practice from schools and teachers who are known to be effective, it is another matter altogether to set about trying to change the existing practice of all teachers. Fullan (1999) in a review of the factors that can contribute to the success of large-scale reform acknowledges the difficulty of implementing and sustaining change across a large number of schools.

> . . . none of the programs can be made teacher-proof, school-proof, or district-proof. Indifference, negative climate, neglect of implementation training and support, such as program-specific staff development, and failure to build-in systems and time for co-ordination and problem solving could kill implementation of any program.
>
> (Fullan, 1999: 11)

He concludes, however, that positive effects are possible, particularly where the systems and the structures are well-supported through resources, staff development and commitment on the part of educators and the public at large. It is interesting, though, that the review is all about systems and structures and not about the particularity of the individual context; but for large-scale reform to be successful each part of the whole has to share the understanding.

Leithwood *et al.* (1999) in part of the first annual report of the external evaluation of the NLS/NNS, review evidence for what works in successfully implementing and sustaining reform. They consider three elements: will, capacity and infrastructure. In all of these it is the institutional will, capacity and infrastructure that is addressed at length. Individual capacity receives the briefest treatment, although the importance of influencing each member of the teaching community is acknowledged. The authors recognise the difficulties of attaining a 'reasonably uniform, widespread understanding of a single reform initiative, especially one consistent with what its development had in mind . . .' (p. 15).

The concept of a nation-wide reform of teaching is one that is fraught with difficulties. Whilst a procedure can be laid down and objectives set, there is no guarantee that this will bring about pedagogical change. Studies of teacher development and teaching style suggest that teachers do not readily take on new teaching methods and are slow to change their ways of teaching (e.g. Desforges and Cockburn, 1987; Tharp and Gallimore, 1988; Galton *et al.*, 1999). Hoffman (1998) in a paper entitled 'When bad things happen to good ideas in literacy education' considers the nature of change, innovation and professionalism in literacy education. He contends that innovations are transformed through practice – often from good to bad.

The problem with teaching

The NLS has laid down the classroom organisational structures, the teaching approaches, and the teaching intentions that should be covered in each term. Although implementation is underway, pupils' learning is affected not only by organisation and content but by how these are translated by teachers through the complex patterns of interaction in the primary classroom. The NLS describes procedures and content for working with classes of pupils, but each class is made up of individual children who often confound the best laid plans.

The studies of school and teacher effectiveness considered above relate to what Willinsky (1990) describes as a 'pedagogy of proficiency' (p. 162). In fact, classrooms and teachers do not always operate proficiently – not because of any clear deficiency in themselves but because of the nature of the task itself. Woods (1986) discusses the complex nature of pedagogical knowledge. He describes this as the knowledge that informs and constitutes the action of teaching, involving the whole circumstances surrounding the task. It is informed by theory from a variety of areas: philosophy (why it is done), psychology (how children learn), sociology (knowledge of the social factors affecting learning) and linguistics (communication). Cook-Gumperz (1986) stresses, 'Literacy learning takes place in a social environment through intellectual exchanges in which what is to be learned is to some extent a joint construction of teacher and student' (p. 8). This view of teaching is much harder to reconcile with a model that prescribes the content and format of lessons. In addition, the teacher's own model of teaching will influence the way in which she teaches. Teachers who see literacy teaching as essentially the transmission of skills will teach the NLS in a very different way from a teacher who is responsive to the individual child and views literacy as a complex interaction between what the learner already knows and that which is to be learned.

National Literacy Strategy

Perhaps the key change in teaching required by the NLS is the importance afforded to direct instruction. The Framework for Teaching asserts,

> The literacy hour offers a structure of classroom management, designed to maximise the time teachers spend directly teaching their class. It is intended to shift the balance of teaching from individualised work, especially in the teaching of reading, towards more whole class and group teaching.
>
> (DfEE, 1998: 10)

Since 1992 and the 'Three Wise Men Report' (Alexander *et al.*, 1992) there has been pressure to reduce the amount of individualised teaching in primary schools. This was in response to research into school and teacher effectiveness which showed direct instruction to be effective (e.g. Brophy and Good, 1986) and studies in England on classroom practices that considered the management implications for the individual approach adopted by most primary teachers. As early as 1981, Southgate *et al.*, reported on the Extending Beginning Reading Project (Southgate *et al.*, 1981) that found teachers of 8- and 9-year-old children spent more time dealing with procedural matters than interacting with children about their reading or writing. Bennett *et al.* (1984) also found teachers to be spending time hearing individuals read while attending to other matters. They criticised what they describe as an air of, 'crisis management' in classrooms with teachers trying to interact individually with children most of the time. Ironically, Tizard *et al.* (1988) found that, in the classes of teachers who spent most time listening to individual children read, pupils themselves spent least time engaged in reading. Ofsted (1995) also criticised the management of the teaching of reading and argued that teachers could manage time more effectively. Whilst appropriate response and interaction with individuals is important, there clearly were difficulties for primary teachers who were trying to teach a full curriculum at the same time as working with each child individually.

Theories of learning

Research also points to the importance of starting with what the learner already knows (Ausubel, 1968); of providing appropriate learning activities (Vygotsky, 1962; Bruner and Haste, 1987); of the capacity of the teacher to ensure high-quality interaction (Galton *et al.*, 1980; Edwards and Mercer, 1987). Strangely absent from Beard's Review of Research and Related Evidence for the National Literacy Strategy is any mention of theories of learning. Although the key elements of the hour: shared and guided reading and writing are explained and authors who have written about these approaches are cited, there is no consideration of the theories of learning underpinning these.

   Research into how children learn (Vygotsky, 1962, 1978; Bruner, 1977, 1983; Donaldson, 1978) has led us to believe the following:

- Children are actively concerned with making sense of their worlds and talk underpins this active reconstruction.
- Learning is a shared activity which takes place within the cultural and social context.
- Children will learn more in co-operation with adults or peers than might be thought possible from their Piagetian stage of development.
- The child learns in close association with a caring adult.

Two of Vygotsky's (1962 and 1978) main propositions concern the centrality of language and the importance of shared social behaviour. His fundamental premise is that development takes place within social and cultural settings. Related to this is the importance of the adult or more experienced 'other' who can help the child develop within the zone of proximal development. The implications of this for teaching are great. If speech in childhood lays the foundations for a lifetime of thinking, talk in the classroom is essential. If shared social behaviour is seen as the source of learning, there are further implications for the teacher's role. It is the interaction that takes place between adult and learner in the context of learning that is central to that learning.

Wells (1987) showed the difficulties of achieving this in a busy classroom but interaction between teacher and child(ren), and child and child is essential. The Piagetian notion of children as 'lone scientists' is no longer tenable. Teachers need to find ways to maximise the opportunities for interaction in their classrooms and ways of supporting the child's development. However, we must recognise that the nature of that interaction will determine the learner's view of learning: whether the interaction is geared to pacey delivery and achievement of objectives or whether it is designed to encourage reflection and exploration.

Bruner is one of the most notable contemporary exponents of the view that language develops in children through processes of social interaction. In Bruner's (1983) theory of the development of knowledge the human being is regarded as an active creator and learner. Bruner regards language as a tool and considers how the child learns through interaction with adults to use the tool effectively and efficiently. He believes that for learning to take place appropriate social interactional frameworks must be provided – he called these 'scaffolding' (Bruner, 1977). In early language development the parent, usually the mother, provides the framework which allows the child to learn. To do this she provides contexts and routines that are familiar to the child. She remains finely tuned to the capabilities of her child and lets him/her proceed at an appropriate pace supported by her use of language to lead and extend her child's development. This notion of 'scaffolding' is central to shared reading and writing. Here the teacher models the reading or writing process and takes the role of the expert allowing the child to read or write at a level beyond that which they could achieve on their own. This theory is a powerful one but the whole class group is clearly a very different context from the individual child with a parent.

Research also reminds us that learners learn about literacy in different ways. There have been criticisms that holistic approaches to literacy teaching are based on research in white middle-class settings, whereas evidence is accruing that children from different home backgrounds learn in different ways (Heath, 1983; Mason, 1992; Reyes 1992; Anderson, 1995).

Donaldson (1978) presented a picture of children who are active and efficient learners. She discussed how children are actively making sense of the situations in which they find themselves and also that, where children can put the problem presented within their own frame of reference, they can do much more than would be expected from their Piagetian stage of development. Effective use of shared and guided reading can enable children to make sense of the skills they are being taught in the context of an authentic piece of text as opposed to decontextualised exercises which have been evident in the past.

Model of teaching

The model of literacy instruction adopted by the NLS owes a good deal to the approach adopted in New Zealand (Bickler, 1999; Sylva *et al.,* 1999). In this there is a careful balance between teacher instruction and pupil effort. Figure 1.1 illustrates the relationship between various parts of the literacy lesson and the locus of the 'effort'. This balance is fundamental to the programme of shared, guided and independent work that makes up the literacy hour. In shared work, the teacher plays the largest part and leads the interaction, scaffolding the learning. In guided work, the children are encouraged to be independent but the teacher supports their independence through focused and targeted instruction. In independent work, children are primarily working independently and practising or exploring what they have already been taught. If this is understood it can provide a balanced experience for children in which the teacher teaches but where they also have opportunities to explore for themselves.

However, direct instruction for some people conjures up a view of literacy teaching that sees literacy as no more than a set of skills to be transmitted to the learner. In the words of Geekie *et al.* (1999), those who advocate systematic and explicit instruction

> believe that learning involves a transmission of knowledge and skills from teacher to learner, with the teacher determining what is to be learnt, and in what order. And what is being learnt is a set of skills, demonstrated by an expert, and mastered through repeated practice of the component skills.
>
> (Geekie *et al.,* 1999: 3)

In contrast, they argue that children are social beings who are constantly engaged with other people in making sense of their world experience. Thus, it is inappropriate to start with the premise that the human mind is essentially a processor of information. Langer (1997) warns against teaching that encourages the development of nonconscious automaticity. Cambourne (1999) extends this to the need for a 'metacognitive awareness: that is the state of being consciously aware of what's going on' (p. 127). Wood (1986)

The literacy hour is intended to promote 'literacy instruction' but this is not a recipe for returning to some crude or simple form of 'transmission' teaching. The most successful teaching is:

- discursive – characterised by high quality oral work;
- interactive – pupils' contributions are encouraged, expected and extended;
- well-paced – there is a sense of urgency, driven by the need to make progress and succeed;
- confident – teachers have a clear understanding of the objectives;
- ambitious – there is optimism about and high expectations of success.

(DfEE, 1998: 8)

However, the way these descriptions of practice are implemented in the classroom may be influenced more by the teacher's own view of learning than by the descriptions of practice presented by the NLS training materials. Our research showed that teachers adopted the NLS to a large extent in line with the guidelines but that the way they interacted with their pupils and the activities they chose as contexts for their teaching were still very different and may have contributed to the differential progress made by children in the project classrooms.

Cambourne (1999) in a critique of the movement to 'explicit and systematic' teaching of literacy considers what this means and concludes that there is nothing wrong with explicit and systematic teaching but that

> It is when explicit and systematic teaching is also mindless and decontextualised that it becomes dangerous because it makes learning much more complex than it ought to be . . . contextualised teaching that is also implicit and unsystematic would also create serious barriers for many learners.

(Cambourne, 1999: 127)

Thus it is the way in which the teacher manages the tensions implicit in the system that will make the difference. It is in the achievement of a balance between what is to be taught and how it is learned that success will be found.

Implementation of the National Literacy Strategy

The NLS was introduced into English primary schools in September 1998. Most people in one way or another agreed there was a need to, either or both, raise literacy standards and to support teachers in the management of the teaching of literacy. Many educational commentators questioned the lack of research evidence to justify such a massive commitment (Goldstein,

1997; Sweetman, 1998; Wragg, 1998), yet Beard's (1999) review presented an impressive range of evidence to support the content and structure of the NLS. Despite this, questions have been raised about the feasibility of changing teacher practice on such a large and externally imposed scale.

National test results

Results from the first 18 months of the National Literacy Project (NLP) were promising (Sainsbury *et al.*, 1998) and the wholesale implementation of the NLS in all English primary schools followed on from this early success. However, in the case of the NLP, the project had been targeted in those areas where the need was considered highest. Initial results from national tests were encouraging. Overall attainment at Level 4 or above in English for 11-year-olds increased by 10 percentage points in the first two years of the NLS. There was also an increase in the proportion of children achieving Level 5. Although the increase in attainment at Key Stage 1 was smaller, 6 per cent more children achieved Level 2b in reading and 8 per cent more in writing, there has been very little change in the proportion of children reaching Level 3 in reading or writing (DfEE, 2000a).

Ofsted evaluation

HMI were charged with the monitoring of the impact of the NLS in schools up to the key date of 2002. They claim, undoubtedly correctly, that 'The NLS continues to have a major impact on the teaching of English in primary schools. . . . The teaching of reading in primary schools has undergone a transformation' (Ofsted, 2000b: para. 5). They go on to comment on the amount of 'effective whole-class work at both key stages' which has had a positive effect on standards of pupils' reading. However, they report that the impact on writing has been limited. In both of the reports of the first two years they report that children's attitudes to the literacy hour are good (Ofsted, 1999 and 2000a).

External evaluation

It could be argued that national assessment and inspection procedures were more than likely to produce positive results since each adhere to the same model of literacy and of teaching. The team from Ontario under Michael Fullan was less positive in their claims for the success of the National Literacy and Numeracy Strategy (NLNS). After the first year of monitoring they agreed that modest but significant gains had been made in literacy and numeracy but argue that it would be naïve to claim these were all due to the NLNS (Earl *et al.*, 2000). They cite other factors such as increased motivation and effort to explain short-term gains. 'Continued achievement gains will depend on teachers learning new skills – a slow incremental process' (p. 7). They claim that their research indicates that, after 18 months 'it is too soon to tell the extent to which these practices are being integrated into the routine work of schools and the feasibility of doing so' (p. 6).

Surprisingly, little empirical research was reported in the first two years of the NLS. What little evidence there was indicated that teachers, on the whole, welcomed the literacy strategy (Dadds, 1999; Beverton and English, 1999; Fisher and Lewis, 1999). However, despite the apparent increase in attainment, early reports of research into classroom interaction raised serious questions about the quality of the interaction taking place between teachers and children in the literacy hour. Mroz et al. (2000) in an analysis of the classroom discourse of ten literacy hours found that both whole class and guided work sessions were essentially teacher dominated.

> Because of the teachers' claim to prior knowledge of the subject content, and right to control the pacing and sequencing of its transmission, pupils rarely managed to impose their own relevance outside the teachers' frame of reference. . . . In all 10 lessons the teacher was predominantly seen to be retaining control over the direction and pace of the lesson and the lines of knowledge which were to be pursued.
>
> (Mroz et al., 2000: 382)

Similar concerns were raised by Moyles et al. (2000) in an early report of a project examining how primary teachers conceptualise and utilise interactive teaching. Interviews with teachers showed that they were facing dilemmas in trying to implement interactive teaching strategies in a way that reconciled their own theories of teaching and their practice within the prescribed format of the NLS. The early findings from this project suggest that although some teachers seemed aware of the importance of a focus on thinking and learning strategies, none explicitly described teaching methods intended to enhance pupil thinking and learning or achieve the NLS goal of the development of higher order thinking.

This evidence seems to indicate the difficulties teachers are having reconciling child-centred ideologies with an objectives-led curriculum.

Conclusion

In order to develop/improve teaching we need to be clear about the model that is proposed. Beard (1999) is strangely silent on this. His review explains and justifies the content of the Framework and the format of the hour. He reviews research on effective teaching but the model of the teacher remains invisible. Even where strategies such as shared and guided reading and writing are considered, the evidence of how they are implemented and how successful they have been is reviewed but there is no mention of underlying principles. Research shows that individual teachers influence the success of any programme and that it is likely to be the way they respond to and interact with individuals that makes that difference. Contingent teaching, as described by Wood (1986), provides the interface between teacher and learner. This cannot be achieved through a prescribed format of timed sections and specified objectives. The success of the literacy strategy depends on the individual teachers.

The intention of this book is to provide detailed and rich descriptions of the practice of successful teachers in the literacy hour in order to inform teachers and those who work with them. The teachers in our study, like other teachers around the country, were given training days by members of their own staff through a cascade model of professional development. This involved some discussion and watching video material showing teachers teaching parts of the literacy hour. Most particularly, in the early videos, the emphasis was on management of routines. There was no discussion of underlying theories of learning; no opportunities for teachers to relate their own theories to the new theory; no opportunities for the literacy co-ordinator with her carefully planned script to engage the teachers in high-quality interaction about the literacy hour; in fact, there was no opportunity for contingent teaching.

It seems that early evidence of the implementation of the NLS suggested considerable change in the organisation and management of the teaching of literacy in primary school classrooms. Evidence from national tests indicates some significant gains in attainment. However, as with previous innovations, implementation varied across the range of schools and teachers. Unsurprisingly the NLS has provided no panacea. The success of the teaching of literacy still seems to depend to a large extent on the individual teacher and how that teacher interacts with the individual children in her class. The purpose of this book is to look at the rich descriptive detail revealed by our research into twenty classrooms during the literacy hour and to try to describe what has seemed to be effective teaching of literacy.

2 The research project

Introduction

In this chapter I want to describe the background to the project and offer some evaluation of its validity and reliability. I will explain our aims and objectives, our methods and how we collected and analysed the data. Those readers who want to go straight to the analysis of classrooms can leave this chapter out and go on to the next. There will be enough in each chapter to explain where the findings came from and you can always come back to read this later if you wish.

Background

The project, funded by ESRC, ran over one year from the introduction of the NLS in most primary schools in England. The main part of the funding was spent on the employment of a research assistant for 16 months to cover data collection and initial analysis. A second phase to the research involved a follow-up visit to twelve of the project classrooms at the end of the second year of the NLS in order to ascertain how teachers had moved on since the end of the funded project.

The project was set in a rural area of England where there are many small schools with mixed-age classes. The emphasis placed in the NLS on focused objectives for each term in each year presented a problem to teachers of mixed-age classes who could have as many as four different year groups in one class. As the year progressed, however, it became apparent that most of the issues encountered by the project teachers had direct relevance to all teachers and were not restricted to small schools.

The National Foundation for Educational Research had been commissioned by government to conduct research into the effectiveness of the National Literacy Project, a *post-hoc* pilot for the Literacy Strategy. Early evidence from this had shown good results with children from disadvantaged areas (Sainsbury *et al.*, 1998). The Office for Standards in Education (Ofsted) was monitoring the implementation of the Strategy within the normal inspection framework and with visits specifically for observation of the literacy hour. In addition, an international team under Michael Fullan was to report on the implementation of the NLS. We felt there was also needed a more qualitative inquiry into the day to day working of the NLS.

Aims and objectives

The overall aim of the project was to identify the problems, issues and possible solutions that arose from implementing a literacy hour within small rural schools. In order to do this we identified the following research questions:

1   How do teachers in small rural schools implement the literacy hour?
2   What problems do they encounter in managing the literacy hour?
3   What strategies do they employ to overcome these problems?
4   What reasons do they give for the modifications they make?
5   Which classes make good progress in literacy over the first year of teaching a literacy hour?
6   What strategies have teachers in these successful classes used in teaching a literacy hour?
7   What guidelines could be given to other teachers in mixed-age classes to support their teaching of the literacy hour?

Thus our objectives for the project were:

- To measure the effect of the introduction of a literacy hour in small rural schools on pupils' literacy learning through standardised tests and case study evidence.
- Through observation and interview, to identify and analyse the strategies teachers used to teach a literacy hour to suit their classroom situation.
- To identify reasons for these modifications.
- To analyse ways in which teachers have attempted to overcome difficulties in implementation of the literacy hour and identify successful strategies.

Inevitably, with a research project of this kind we only went part way to fulfilling our aims and objectives. We certainly felt we had gained very useful insights into the project classrooms. Our respect for the teachers grew as the year progressed. Whether they were enthusiastic or not about the NLS, they put every effort into trying to make it work for their pupils. Despite the pressure they were under they were always welcoming to our research assistant, even though this sometimes meant moving the timing of the literacy hour when arrangements had gone awry. Measuring the effect of the literacy hour was always going to be problematic and it was only possible to gain some indications of how much progress had been made.

The children

Standardised reading tests

All pupils were tested at the beginning and end of the year using standard-ised reading tests. The tests used were the same ones that had been used by the NFER in the evaluation of the first cohort of the National Literacy Project (Sainsbury *et al.*, 1998). In reception (4/5-year-olds) the *Language and Reading Readiness Test of Emergent Literacy* (LARR) was used on both occasions. In Key Stage 1 the *Primary Reading Test* (PRT) was used: in October as a word recognition test and in June as a comprehension test. At Key Stage 2 the *Progress in English* (PIE) tests were used: Test 8 in October and 9 in June for years 3 and 4; Test 10 in October and 11 in June for years 5 and 6. These tests, while generally accepted as useful measures, focus mainly on reading, although PIE also has a spelling component. The period between tests was shorter than we had originally planned. This was due partly to the late starting of the project because of a delay in the confirmation of funding, and partly to a decision made by the research team that the final round of testing should begin in June in order to ensure that all schools were able to complete tests within the academic year. This meant that the period over which progress was measured was only eight months.

Target children

In order to look more closely at what children in the classes were doing in the literacy hour and to judge their progress in writing, we chose one child from each year group in each class for further observation. Using the information gained from the first reading tests, we identified the child whose standardised test was nearest to 100. Where there was a choice of more than one, we opted for a balance of boys and girls in each class. As well as the observations of the teacher during the literacy hour, the observer made brief notes about each target child's involvement in each part of the lesson (see Appendix III).

Work samples

We collected written work samples from these target pupils for each month of the project. These work samples consisted of mainly what teachers chose to give us. Mostly they were free writing samples, which gave indications of how children had progressed as writers during the year. Occasionally, we were also given samples of activities used in inde-pendent work during the literacy hour. These provided useful examples of the kind of tasks, other than free writing that children were doing during this time.

Analysis

The analysis and results from the project are discussed in greater detail in the relevant chapters. Qualitative methods of analysis were used mainly. Some statistical analysis was used on the reading tests.

'Teachers' Beliefs about Literacy Questionnaire'

This was analysed in accordance with the guidelines (Westwood *et al.*, 1997). Teachers were rated both according to their responses and according to their own self-rating. We also looked to see how consistent teachers were in their replies in favour of either a child-centred or skills based approach.

Observations and interview data

Ongoing analysis in the first few months of the project involved open coding of the observational and interview data. From this we identified emerging themes, such as use of objectives, pace and expectations. These themes arose partly from our scrutiny of the data and meetings of the research team but also from our own pre-conceptions that led us to look for evidence of those elements of practice which we had expected to observe. In particular we were aware of the findings of teacher effectiveness research and the key features of successful teaching identified by the NLS. It had also become apparent that the observer's strength lay in her sensitivity to children's engagement. While there was evidence of many elements of teacher behaviour, there were some elements that needed further investigation. Thus for the last three visits, in addition to the ongoing observation, the observer looked for evidence of pace, use of routines and metacognitive modelling.

When the evidence from the reading tests and target children had been analysed, further analysis took place of those teachers whose children appeared to have made good progress to try to identify aspects of practice that may have contributed to this progress.

Reading tests

Full details of the analysis of the test data can be found in Chapter 4, where evidence of children's progress in reading is discussed. Although around 400 children were involved in the study, their ages ranged from 4 to 11 years of age. This meant that different tests had to be used for different age groups. Therefore the number of children in each test group was too small to use sophisticated statistical analyses such as multilevel modelling. This had never been our intention. Our view of literacy learning was such that: (1) we did not feel that reading tests gave us a sufficiently full picture of progress in reading to want to make substantive claims from

Introducing the hour

One of the features of teachers' comments as reported by the press before the implementation of the NLS was the fact that they focused, unsurprisingly, on the practicalities of the programme. Teachers were concerned about content, resources and the actual structure of the hour. The educational press, as well as referring to these aspects, expressed concern about the lack of research evidence that such a programme might work. Nowhere in all that was written at the time was there discussion of pedagogical principles. Nowhere was there exploration of the model of teaching. The in-service materials that were sent to all schools by the end of the summer term, 1998, concentrated on the organisation and management of the hour (DfEE, 1998). They gave teachers things to do and left little time for consideration of why certain approaches might be made and how the strategies might fit with teachers' existing teaching style. Even later, when Beard (1999) brought out his retrospective analysis of the research evidence underpinning the NLS, this took each part of the hour's content and structure and considered where it came from. There was no analysis of the whole. In the training materials, teachers were exhorted to make traffic-light signs to help with independent work; to use post-it notes in shared reading; to write their objectives on the black/whiteboard and so on. Unsurprisingly there was little time left for reflection on the way in which the elements of the hour fitted together into a coherent teaching approach.

In fact, the first in-service training module that all schools were expected to cover before leaving for their summer holidays focused predominately on the procedure and management of the hour. Video clips were shown of teachers doing shared and guided reading and writing. Various management strategies were demonstrated to enable children to work independently and for many teachers the lasting impression of this video was the teacher who, having set the tasks for her class, called 'Action!', upon which the pupils quietly filed away to sit at their tables and work busily. Nowhere in this introduction to the NLS was there an explanation of the pedagogical theory. There was 5 minutes at the start of the 5½ hour training day to look at the rationale for the NLS and a further 5 minutes later on in the day when one of two OHTs to be shown in a 5-minute slot outlined what high-quality teaching should entail. Possible teaching strategies were covered briefly but without any chance for discussion or explanation for the reasons why these strategies might be more effective than others. It seemed to be expected that teachers would be able to either map their existing style on to the new framework, or just change their teaching following a few in-service sessions. This seems to run counter to research evidence that shows that teachers' craft knowledge is a composite of their past experiences (Brown and McIntyre, 1993). This is not to imply that the theory should precede the practice – there is as much evidence that shows this does not work either (e.g. Desforges and Cockburn, 1987).

Analysis

The analysis and results from the project are discussed in greater detail in the relevant chapters. Qualitative methods of analysis were used mainly. Some statistical analysis was used on the reading tests.

'Teachers' Beliefs about Literacy Questionnaire'

This was analysed in accordance with the guidelines (Westwood *et al.*, 1997). Teachers were rated both according to their responses and according to their own self-rating. We also looked to see how consistent teachers were in their replies in favour of either a child-centred or skills based approach.

Observations and interview data

Ongoing analysis in the first few months of the project involved open coding of the observational and interview data. From this we identified emerging themes, such as use of objectives, pace and expectations. These themes arose partly from our scrutiny of the data and meetings of the research team but also from our own pre-conceptions that led us to look for evidence of those elements of practice which we had expected to observe. In particular we were aware of the findings of teacher effectiveness research and the key features of successful teaching identified by the NLS. It had also become apparent that the observer's strength lay in her sensitivity to children's engagement. While there was evidence of many elements of teacher behaviour, there were some elements that needed further investigation. Thus for the last three visits, in addition to the ongoing observation, the observer looked for evidence of pace, use of routines and metacognitive modelling.

When the evidence from the reading tests and target children had been analysed, further analysis took place of those teachers whose children appeared to have made good progress to try to identify aspects of practice that may have contributed to this progress.

Reading tests

Full details of the analysis of the test data can be found in Chapter 4, where evidence of children's progress in reading is discussed. Although around 400 children were involved in the study, their ages ranged from 4 to 11 years of age. This meant that different tests had to be used for different age groups. Therefore the number of children in each test group was too small to use sophisticated statistical analyses such as multilevel modelling. This had never been our intention. Our view of literacy learning was such that: (1) we did not feel that reading tests gave us a sufficiently full picture of progress in reading to want to make substantive claims from these tests; and (2) we did not believe that children's progress in reading would be only attributable to what happened in the literacy hour. For these, and the reasons given earlier in this chapter, we opted for a sufficiently small sample to give greater detail of teacher behaviour. Thus the tests provided only some indication of success.

Target children

In all there were 53 target children, one from each year group in each class. Full details of the analysis of the writing samples can be found in Chapter 5 where children's progress in writing is examined. Observations were made of target children's behaviour in each section of each literacy hour. We analysed children's behaviour in an impressionist way to get a feeling for the level of involvement in each class. We also coded the behaviour on a scale of 0 to 3 in order to make some comparison between teachers and between age groups. Where the target child was inattentive at the point of observation, no score was given. If they were fidgeting, they were given 1. If they were attentive but not contributing, they were given 2 and, if they were contributing, they were given 3. This gave a possible score of between 0 and 12 for each literacy hour. This was clearly no more than a guide to children's engagement. A child who was fidgeting at the point of observation did not necessarily indicate that they were not thinking about the lesson. A brief contribution did not necessarily indicate full engagement. Nevertheless, we felt this gave us a reasonable guide to how children were responding to the literacy hour.

In general, we felt most satisfied with the observational and interview data. Although this is, of course, open to criticisms of subjectivity, we feel that it gives a useful, illustrative picture of the literacy hours as they were taught in the first year of implementation. Having three members of the research team meant that discussion was possible, and regular reviewing of the emerging themes.

The initial findings were presented to the teachers from the project at a conference six months after the final visit. There was general agreement that we had presented a generally accurate picture of their classrooms and they were able to add further reflections at this later date.

Validity and reliability

Validity is an important issue in any research project. Researchers want to be able to claim that their methods of data collection are valid ways of gaining insight into the question. In order to ensure, as far as is possible, that our findings were valid we collected evidence from a range of sources:

- Observation by a research assistant who was also a teacher and who could give an informed commentary.

- An open observation schedule that limited as little as possible the scope of the observations.
- Observations over a period of time to try to get a representative picture of the teacher and limit disturbance from observer effect.
- As many as twenty teachers to avoid, to some extent, criticism that our sample was too particular.
- Questionnaire data to give insight into the teachers' beliefs about literacy teaching.
- Interview data that provided insight into teachers' views.
- A semi-structured interview format to allow teachers the chance to expand on the points raised.
- Collection of work samples and observations of target children in each class to provide a fuller picture.
- Reading test data of all children in the project to provide further information.

Of course, many of these factors, while contributing to the validity of the study, raised questions about reliability:

- Having a teacher as a research assistant gave rise to greater risk of observer bias as she already had her own views about the teaching of literacy.
- The openness of the observation schedule did not provide a base line of items to observe.
- The reduction of observer effect as the researcher became known to teacher and children, and vice versa, gave rise to concern that a halo effect could come into operation. This could cause favoured teachers to receive more favourable comments and the researcher to focus more on other teachers' less favoured behaviours.
- The semi-structured interview format could allow teachers to be led in opposing directions according to the whim of the interviewer.
- Observation of children and evaluation of work samples are necessarily subjective activities in which another observer might give different weight to different aspects of the behaviour and/or writing.
- The smallness of the sample in each year group for the reading tests could result in too much weight being attributed to one child's performance on a particular day which may, in fact, have been atypical.

Any interpretation of data is open to alternative interpretation by other observers or readers. Whereas one observer may interpret a child shouting out a response as an act of misbehaviour another may interpret it as active involvement in the lesson. Each interpretation is possible but one would give rise to very different conclusions from the other. We opted for a mixture of means of data collection to provide different perspectives on what constituted success in the literacy hour. This was important as only

Introducing the hour

One of the features of teachers' comments as reported by the press before the implementation of the NLS was the fact that they focused, unsurprisingly, on the practicalities of the programme. Teachers were concerned about content, resources and the actual structure of the hour. The educational press, as well as referring to these aspects, expressed concern about the lack of research evidence that such a programme might work. Nowhere in all that was written at the time was there discussion of pedagogical principles. Nowhere was there exploration of the model of teaching. The in-service materials that were sent to all schools by the end of the summer term, 1998, concentrated on the organisation and management of the hour (DfEE, 1998). They gave teachers things to do and left little time for consideration of why certain approaches might be made and how the strategies might fit with teachers' existing teaching style. Even later, when Beard (1999) brought out his retrospective analysis of the research evidence underpinning the NLS, this took each part of the hour's content and structure and considered where it came from. There was no analysis of the whole. In the training materials, teachers were exhorted to make traffic-light signs to help with independent work; to use post-it notes in shared reading; to write their objectives on the black/whiteboard and so on. Unsurprisingly there was little time left for reflection on the way in which the elements of the hour fitted together into a coherent teaching approach.

In fact, the first in-service training module that all schools were expected to cover before leaving for their summer holidays focused predominately on the procedure and management of the hour. Video clips were shown of teachers doing shared and guided reading and writing. Various management strategies were demonstrated to enable children to work independently and for many teachers the lasting impression of this video was the teacher who, having set the tasks for her class, called 'Action!', upon which the pupils quietly filed away to sit at their tables and work busily. Nowhere in this introduction to the NLS was there an explanation of the pedagogical theory. There was 5 minutes at the start of the 5½ hour training day to look at the rationale for the NLS and a further 5 minutes later on in the day when one of two OHTs to be shown in a 5-minute slot outlined what high-quality teaching should entail. Possible teaching strategies were covered briefly but without any chance for discussion or explanation for the reasons why these strategies might be more effective than others. It seemed to be expected that teachers would be able to either map their existing style on to the new framework, or just change their teaching following a few in-service sessions. This seems to run counter to research evidence that shows that teachers' craft knowledge is a composite of their past experiences (Brown and McIntyre, 1993). This is not to imply that the theory should precede the practice – there is as much evidence that shows this does not work either (e.g. Desforges and Cockburn, 1987).

The impact of this was evident from early in the first term of the project. There was a group of teachers who got down to teaching literacy hours with a will, but whose focus was primarily on the hour. We called this group the 'clock watchers'. They talked about the difficulty of fitting each part of the hour neatly into the lesson. Their changeover from one part of the hour to the other was often rushed or abrupt. Other teachers seemed to work more to make their lessons coherent, to think of ways to make the whole more than just the '15, 15, 20, 10' that Ted Wragg mocked in one of his articles in the *Times Educational Supplement* (Wragg, 1998). Ofsted (1999) also found that 'the best teaching was seen when the fundamentals of good teaching were applied to the literacy hour' (p. 4). Although by the end of the second year teachers no longer talked about timing difficulties, there was still a sense of constraint voiced by some teachers.

Implementation of the hour

We visited each classroom eight times during the first year, and saw one hour of literacy teaching each time. The layout of the observation schedule allowed us to record what the teacher was doing at seven predetermined points during the hour to coincide with the literacy hour structure. This enabled us to judge the extent to which the structure of the hour was being followed on each visit. Of the 158 hours we observed in the first year, 126 had each element of the whole class parts of the hour in place. Of the twenty classes, seven teachers chose to do a complete literacy hour for every visit and a further five did so on seven of the eight visits (see Table 3.1). The remaining eight teachers will be discussed later in this chapter. We were also able to judge how much this was representative of each

Table 3.1   Observed use of the literacy hour in research classrooms

Pupils	Total no. of observ-ations	No. of whole text sessions observed	No. of word/ sentence sessions observed	No. of guided sessions observed	No. of indepen-dent sessions observed	No. of plenary sessions observed
4–7 years Key Stage 1	80	78	71	79/160[a] 45 reading 34 writing	79	73
7–11 years Key Stage 2	78	78	70	40/78 25 reading 15 writing	78	72

Notes: [a]In 80 observed sessions with the younger children (Key Stage 1), 160 guided sessions could have been observed, as teachers of the younger children are expected to work with two guided groups in the 20-minute slot. Thirteen such 'double sessions' were observed in the 80 observations, and 53 'single sessions'.

teacher's practice by looking at their lesson plans and by talking to them during and at the end of the year.

Use of shared work – text level

It can be seen from Table 3.1 that the first quarter of an hour of the literacy hour was the most regularly used by our teachers during the year. Holdaway (1979) promoted the use of enlarged text which teachers and pupils read together. Since then there has been an explosion in the production of 'big books' of a range of genres, from picture books to information texts. Teachers readily adopted these books and shared reading in the NLS was well received. The teachers in our study mentioned this in the end of year interviews as one of the best aspects of the literacy hour. We found shared writing to be less widely used, although this is based on similar principles of modelling the literacy process. Here the teacher demonstrates composition of a text or teacher and pupils jointly construct a text, with the teacher acting as lead and scribe.

Looking more closely at what happened in these literacy hours, we could see that the quality of practice within this part of the hour varied even after two years. Within the framework of children moving from dependent to independent literacy users, shared work gives children, of any ability, the opportunity to enjoy texts that they would not be able to read or write on their own. Having an enlarged version of the text in front of them lets children see what the expert reader or writer does. Teachers can draw attention to aspects of the text or of the reading or writing process. Also, they can say out loud what they are thinking and demonstrate how skilled literacy users think about what they are doing. Only in very few of our classrooms was this in evidence. Often shared reading consisted of no more than teacher and children following a text that was read aloud by the teacher who pointed to the words as she read. There were often several missed opportunities to draw attention to features of the text or the process itself. An example of this can be seen in the extract of shared reading from Mrs Freeman later on in this chapter.

Word level and sentence level

Most teachers implemented the second section of the literacy hour most of the time. On the whole, teachers welcomed the way in which the skills were able to be contextualised by the preceding whole text work. As the year progressed, however, some teachers expressed concern at the way that this part of the hour could dictate the choice of text. It became clear that, while the theory was good, the practicalities of matching word- or sentence-level objectives to the whole text-level work day in day out presented difficulties. It seemed to us to be a healthy sign that teachers sometimes opted to change the positioning of this part of the hour or change the length to ensure a coherent lesson for children. There seemed to be more problems with teachers who slavishly followed the strict format to the detriment of children's learning. In these cases it seemed like four separate lessons were being taught in an hour or poor quality texts were used on a regular basis to ensure coverage of the word- and sentence-level objectives. This problem was recognised by the NLS itself when Progression in Phonics (DfEE, 1999) was brought out in September 1999 which encouraged teachers, if they were going to have their phonics teaching as a stand-alone session, to do it before the whole text work.

Use of guided work

One of the key features of the NLS is the importance given to teachers actually teaching for 100 per cent of the time during the literacy hour. Although in interviews at the end of the year teachers said they had mainly used the literacy hour, our observations show variations from the pre-scribed pattern. These can be seen in Table 3.1. One of the key features of the literacy hour is the 20-minute slot where most of the class works independently and the teacher teaches reading or writing strategies to one small group for 20 minutes (Key Stage 2) or two small groups for 10 minutes each (Key Stage 1). These 20 minutes provide the opportunity for teachers to work on particular areas for development with children of similar levels of attainment. The major difference between the literacy hours observed in the different classes was in this time. In eight of the classes we observed the teacher working with small group(s) on less than three occasions and in only seven of the classes did we see this on a regular basis. At Key Stage 2, we only observed three teachers to use the guided slot regularly and two of these more usually did guided reading. Although only one literacy hour was observed each month, I would argue that, if teachers were not using guided reading or writing when their literacy hours were under observation, it is unlikely that they would use it at other times. Further evidence of the infrequent use of guided work by some of the teachers was found by examination of teachers' weekly planning sheets. Two years after the launch of the NLS a sample of sixty teachers identified guided reading/writing as the most difficult part of the hour to implement (see Chapter 10).

Use of independent work

Developing independence is one of the key features of the literacy strategy, yet there were major differences observed in classrooms during this time. Those teachers who did not use the guided section for group teaching either worked with individual children or moved around the class overseeing the tasks set. They responded to perceived individual needs and answered children's questions. In addition to missing the opportunity to teach small groups, this resulted in the children in these classes being less able to work found setting independent work difficult. There seemed to be little under-standing of the relationship between these three complementary teaching/learning activities.

[Shared reading gives children the chance to 'read' texts that they would not normally be able to read independently.] The teacher, as the expert, reads a text that is beyond most children's ability to read independently. Either by supplying the more difficult words, sustaining interest by use of intonation or enhancing comprehension through careful questioning, the teacher leads the less experienced reader into the world of texts at a level in advance of what they could do on their own. It was clear from the end of year interviews that most teachers and children enjoyed this aspect of the literacy hour but only some teachers seemed to have understood how shared reading fitted into the pattern of teaching in the NLS. Those who did understand referred to the advantage of less able children being able to access a wider range of texts; how it gives all children a chance to say (as opposed to write) their ideas; and how the teacher can boost children's confidence through targeted questioning. Other teachers mentioned the enjoyment and aspects of the procedure (such as covering up words with post-it notes) or expressed concerns about less able children being left behind.

In the guided reading session, the teacher works with a group of children on a text of which they can mostly read about 80 per cent on their own. The teacher guides children by providing some of the more unusual words in the text or directing them to identify the main theme of the text or key strategies that will help them understand. The idea being that this time is for children to be helped to gain independence as readers. In the past, the practice has been for teachers or other adults to listen to children read aloud from a text one at a time. This could be a useful opportunity for assessment or a time to get to know a child as an individual, however, it was not often the occasion for any teaching of reading, was very time-consuming in a large class and did not foster independence.

A literacy hour observed recently during the follow-up project two years after the introduction of the literacy hour showed a teacher still not understanding the different functions of the two parts of the hour. In the first quarter of an hour, she had an enlarged text of a poem; one at a time, children came to the front of the class and read sentences out aloud or answered questions. It was difficult to see what the purpose of this was beyond either a test situation for those who found it difficult or a celebration for those good readers who managed without difficulty. The observer's field notes back up the impression given by the audio-tape of the shared reading session,

> She has chosen a text she likes and she knows will appeal to the children. She gives a lot of attention to interpreting the text for the children and quizzing their understanding of the story as well as

grammar, spelling and punctuation, . . . They are working because of the effective training provided at local level and the management offered centrally by the Standards and Effectiveness Unit.

(DfEE, 2000a)

This seems somewhat overstated since scores at Key Stage 1 had risen only a little and at Key Stage 2 the improvement had started before the introduction of the literacy strategy.

Progress in reading is traditionally measured by standardised tests and this was the means we used. We were aware that there are many shortcomings to this method and that these sort of tests can only be seen as a crude measure of performance. However, they do provide data that are readily comparable. We had wanted to gain some sort of objective measure of teacher success in teaching the literacy strategy that would counterbalance our more subjective judgements of teaching and learning. For further discussion of our methodology, see Chapter 2.

All children in the sample classes were tested at the beginning of the year and again at the end. We decided to ask the teachers to administer the tests themselves because we felt this would give children more of a chance of showing their best. At the beginning of the year, the children and teachers did not know our research assistant, and, although we realised that testing would place an extra burden on teachers, we felt that it would provide a more accurate picture of what children could do.

The tests

The tests chosen were the same as those used by NFER in their evaluation of the first cohort of the National Literacy Project (Sainsbury *et al.*, 1998). This enabled us to compare our sample with the much larger nation-wide sample. Subsequently, NFER opted to develop different measures for the evaluation of the second cohort because of shortcomings found in some of the tests, but the new tests were not available to us at the start of the project.

LARR Test of Emergent Literacy (LARR)

The LARR Test of Emergent Literacy was developed in the early 1980s. It can used with a group and is designed to be used with children when they start school. It is not a test of reading performance but aims to show whether children understand the purpose of the skill they are learning and grasp the concepts needed to talk and think about performing the skill. The LARR test examines whether children can recognise print in various contexts, if they know when reading or writing is taking place and if they understand the basic technical terms associated with reading and writing. It is intended to enable teachers to identify the children who already have well-developed levels of reading and writing knowledge and to pick out children who need to develop further their understanding of the concepts and conventions of print.

Primary Reading Test (PRT)

The Primary Reading Test, developed in the late 1970s, claims to assess children's ability to apply what reading skills they have to the understanding of words and simple sentences in the early stages of learning to read. The test is made up of forty-eight items arranged in ascending levels of difficulty. The items include pictures with five possible words to match, followed by sentences with blanks and five possible words to complete the meaning. This test can be administered as either a word recognition test, in which the items are read to the children and they identify the target word or a comprehension test, in which children read on their own and select the word that best completes the sentence. One problem with this test is that several of the year 1 children in our sample (and several in the NFER sample) were younger than the lowest age in the standardisation table. For this reason we had to estimate scores for these children. This test was given as a word recognition test in October and as a comprehension test in June. The increased difficulty of this version of the test may have accounted for the lack of evident progress made by some children in Key Stage 1 in our sample.

Progress in English (PIE)

Progress in English 8–13, developed in the early 1990s by NFER, is a series of six English language tests covering the age range 7–13+. Tests 8, 9, 10 and 11 were used in this project. PIE8 was used at entry and PIE9 at exit for years 3 and 4 children (age 7–9). PIE10 was used at entry and PIE11 at exit for years 5 and 6 children (age 9–11). These tests are designed to provide teachers with information about a range of language abilities of their pupils. Each test comprises a variety of reading and editing exercises that allow the teacher mainly to assess reading but also elements of spelling, punctuation and grammar. The teacher's guide not only has instructions on how to administer the individual tests but also gives information on how to link a pupil's progress from one test to the next.

Results

October results

Children in each of the twenty classes were given the tests in October, shortly after the beginning of the 1998/9 school year. Children with special educational needs, whose teachers thought they were unlikely to be able to complete the tests, did not take them to avoid the possibility of distress.

The average standardised score across all the tests was 102.79. This meant that the sample was slightly above the national average (100) as indicated by the standardisation statistics. This is in contrast to the NFER sample which, in line with the intentions of the National Literacy Project, contained children from areas where attainment was below the national average. The lowest scoring child in our sample had a standardised score of 70 and the highest had a score of 139. Overall the standard deviation was 13. The mean standardised scores of each of the key stage one classes in the project ranged from 98 to 105, showing very little difference in average attainment – according, at least, to the test scores. There was a greater variation in the mean standardised scores for the key stage two classes, ranging from 95 to 111. The average standardised score and highest and lowest scores can be examined in Table 4.2. These can only give a very general picture as some means have been calculated by averaging scores across more than one test (e.g. LARR and PRT at Key Stage 1) as some classes contained children from more than two year groups.

Table 4.2 Results of the October and June tests for each class

Class	October			June		
	Average standard-ised score[a]	*Lowest score*	*Highest score*	*Average standard-ised score*[a]	*Lowest score*	*Highest score*
Mrs Andrews KS1	102	75	123	101	72	128
Mrs Odgers KS1	99	70	130	98	63	132
Mrs Freeman KS1	100	88	125	98	85	125
Mrs Harman KS1	97	80	118	104	78	128
Mrs Ibbotsen KS1	101	87	123	103	87	122
Mrs Smith KS1[b]	N/A	N/A	N/A	N/A	N/A	N/A
Mrs King KS1	105	92	130	98	75	122
Mrs Channing KS1	103	90	120	109	85	125
Mrs Noakes KS1	105	82	125	112	89	137
Mrs Clark KS1	98	76	120	112	94	132
Mrs York KS2	103	75	123	107	77	135
Mrs David KS2	111	99	139	105	75	131
Mrs Milne KS2	106	85	137	102	75	124
Mrs Graham KS2	102	82	137	109	97	130
Mr Piper KS2	108	84	132	104	82	137
Mrs James KS2	95	79	114	99	77	117
Mrs Burns KS2	104	83	118	101	79	115
Mr Leonard KS2	101	73	134	102	73	121
Mr Ellis KS2	109	88	134	104	76	135
Mrs Quick KS2	102	77	134	101	74	130

Notes: [a]All scores have been rounded to the nearest whole number.
[b]These scores were not counted as the teacher misread the test instructions.

The scores are attributed to the teacher, but it is recognised that other factors, including the input of other teachers will have affected the results. Some teachers were the headteacher and had cover for one or two days in the week. Teachers are named so that readers can identify the classes in the rest of the book.

June test results

Class teachers retested all children in their classes in June 1999, after they had been teaching the literacy hour for nine months. Except for the LARR test for reception children, each of the tests has a second version that is designed to allow retesting. The Primary Reading test was used as a word recognition test in October and as a comprehension test in June. At this round of testing, 380 children were tested in the twenty classes. We did not include the scores of new reception children who had started school after the entry tests in October. The scores from the key stage one class at Sycamore Primary School had to be discounted as we discovered later through discussion with the class teacher that she had administered the more difficult form of the test in October. At this round of testing the average standardised score was 103.8, only a very small increase overall with a standard deviation of 14.02. In June the lowest standardised score was 63 and the highest was 137. The average standardised score and highest and lowest scores for June and October can be examined in Table 4.2.

Progress in reading

We used the same method as NFER to judge the progress made by children and to compare progress in each of the study classrooms. We calculated a progress score by finding the difference between each child's October standardised score and June standardised score. Standardised score gives a score of 100 to a child whose test result is deemed to be average for a child of his/her age on the particular test. Standardised tests such as those used in this study have been trialled on very large numbers of children in different parts of the country in order to obtain a national standard. As the standardisation table caters for monthly differences in age, in theory children should have the same standardised score as the previous test if their performance has not changed any more than would be expected from the passage of time. Three hundred and forty-two children were tested on both occasions and the average progress score for the sample was 1.009 with a standard deviation of 10.85. Given the reasons cited above for expecting slightly suppressed scores in the June sample, we feel confident that overall our sample made, at least, the expected progress over the eight months between tests.

In order to evaluate any possible significance in the differences between the October and June testing, two tailed t-tests were conducted for the scores from each of the different tests. As can be seen from Table 4.3, no significant difference was observed between the two occasions except for the reception children. This is not surprising, given that the period between tests was only eight months and, for all but the reception pupils, the exit test was more difficult being intended for use after one year. The reception children's test covered language and literacy awareness and it is unsur-

Table 4.3   Statistics for reading test scores

Age group		October	June	Paired samples test
Reception	No of valid cases (*n*)	26	26	df = 25
				Sig (2 tailed)=0.019
	Mean	105.3	111.7	
	Standard deviation	9.4	12.2	
Years 1 and 2	No of valid cases (*n*)	102	102	df=101
				Sig (2 tailed)=0.061
	Mean	99.8	102.1	
	Standard deviation	11.7	15.3	
Years 3 and 4	No of valid cases (*n*)	79	79	df=78
				Sig (2 tailed)=0.698
	Mean	101.7	102.1	
	Standard deviation	14.3	13.1	
Years 5 and 6	No of valid cases (*n*)	133	133	df=132
				Sig (2 tailed)=0.778
	Mean	105.2	104.6	
	Standard deviation	13.8	12.8	

prising that after eight months in school with extensive exposure to print these children had made significant progress.

It is not possible to draw conclusions about the effectiveness of the NLS from our sample. Each group is relatively small and there are other reasons that could explain the lack of significant progress. The comprehension version of the PRT test was judged by NFER to be quite a bit more difficult than the word recognition version and therefore they felt their retest scores were lower than expected (Sainsbury *et al.*, 1998). The Progress in English (PIE) tests have different versions for each age group, therefore it was possible to give different tests to each year group. However, it should be noted that only eight months had passed between tests instead of the year for which the tests are designed. This may have resulted in children appearing to make less progress than would have shown had they been tested twelve, instead of eight, months later. We support the view that the national tests for reading give more detailed information of progress over the whole country. Our tests were not intended to measure progress but rather to help us identify teachers who seemed to be using the literacy hour effectively.

More interesting is the distribution of the scores between the classes. When we compared the means for each class, the differences were found to be significant for all but the reception children. This confirmed our impressions from the observational data and writing samples that performance and progress varied considerably between classes. It can be seen from Table 4.4 that some children have made large increases in standardised score over the period whereas others have, in fact, decreased their score by as many as 29 points. Of course, there are many factors that can influence how children perform on tests, such as illness, upset and so on. Equally, children may have made progress in their reading performance as a result

Table 4.4   Progress scores for each class

Class	Average progress score[a]	Lowest progress score	Highest progress score
Mrs Andrews KS1	−1	−27	+24
Mrs Odgers KS1	0	−19	+19
Mrs Freeman KS1	−3	−17	+7
Mrs Harman KS1	+9	−3	+35
Mrs Ibbotsen KS1	+5	−1	+11
Mrs Smith KS1[b]	N/A	N/A	N/A
Mrs King KS1	−5	−28	+19
Mrs Channing KS1	+9	−5	+20
Mrs Noakes KS1	+8	−12	34
Mrs Clark KS1	+11	−5	+35
Mrs York KS2	+5	−1	+15
Mrs David KS2	−8	−24	+4
Mrs Milne KS2	−2	−15	+12
Mrs Graham KS2	+7	−1	+11
Mr Piper KS2	−6	−28	+14
Mrs James KS2	+4	−12	+17
Mrs Burns KS2	−3	−12	+15
Mr Leonard KS2	+3	−21	+25
Mr Ellis KS2	−2	−29	+22
Mrs Quick KS2	−1	−12	+20

Notes: [a]All scores have been rounded to the nearest whole number.
[b]These scores were not counted as the teacher misread the test instructions.

of home or other factors from outside school. Not all increases in stand-ardised scores can be attributed to what the teacher has done during the year. Nevertheless, the large differences in average progress scores between classes is of interest.

In order to examine the possible extent of this difference between the progress scores of the different classes we used one-way analysis of variance to examine the difference (see Table 4.5). There were found to be significant differences between nine of the nineteen classes. Mrs Clark's Key Stage 1 class made significantly more progress than nine of the lower scoring classes, three of which were also Key Stage 1 classes. Mrs Harman's and Mrs Ibbotsen's Key Stage 1 classes made significantly more progress than five of the other classes, although only one of these was a Key Stage 1 class. Mrs David's Key Stage 2 class made significantly less progress than nine other classes, four of which were also Key Stage 2 classes.

Questions

There were many questions raised in our minds by these results. We are fully aware of the limitations of tests such as those taken by the children in our study: that they test only a narrow range of skills and that performance is dependent upon a whole range of personal as well as cognitive

Table 4.5   Analysis of variance between classes

Age group		Sum of squares	df	Mean sqaure	F	Sig
Reception	Between groups (combined)	1,311.789	6	218.633	1.928	0.123
	Within groups	2,381.167	21	113.389		
	Total	3,692.964	27			
Years 1 and 2	Between groups (combined)	5,125.985	8	640.748	6.909	0.000
	Within groups	8,531.659	92	92.735		
	Total	13,657.644	100			
Years 3 and 4	Between groups (combined)	2,755.305	7	393.615	4.853	0.000
	Within groups	5,920.571	73	81.104		
	Total	8,675.877	80			
Years 5 and 6	Between groups (combined)	2,499.719	8	312.465	4.112	0.000
	Within groups	9,421.514	124	75.980		
	Total	11,921.233	132			

factors. Despite this, it is clearly interesting that there are many individual children whose scores have gone down considerably as well as many whose scores have gone up. It is also interesting that there were such differences between the average progress scores in different classes. We began to speculate as to what factors might be associated with good or poor progress. Was there something about particular children or their circumstances that made them less likely to do well? We decided to scrutinise further the data for answers to the following questions:

1   Was there any difference in the performance of boys and girls?
2   Did the size of class make any difference?
3   Did the number of year groups in the class make any difference?
4   Did whether the child was in the oldest or youngest year group in a mixed-age class make any difference?
5   Did the attainment at the start of the year make any difference?

In order to examine these questions we decided to reduce the data to more manageable numbers by grouping the results. Therefore, we put all children's progress scores into three groups: the top third who had made the most progress; a middle third whose scores were around the average; and a lowest third of children whose scores had gone down rather than up. We then used cross-tabulation to consider the percentage of children falling into each group. If there was no difference between the groups you would expect each group to have about 33 per cent of the children in each of the three progress groups.

Was there any difference in the performance of boys and girls?

There were 342 children in the twenty classes, 163 girls and 179 boys. Since there has been growing concern about performance of boys and girls in English over recent years (Ofsted, 1993; QCA, 1998) we expected that the boys would have made less progress than the girls as this would match national trends. In fact there was very little difference between how boys and girls had performed, as can be seen in Table 4.6. Although boys appear to have made slightly less progress overall, the difference is very small and would not explain the differences that we found in progress scores across the sample.

Did the size of class make any difference?

Since our sample was chosen from small rural schools there was a wide range of class sizes, varying from sixteen in the smallest class to thirty-three in the largest class. Obviously during the year numbers varied but the sizes given here are from the autumn term at the start of the project. The smallest classes increased in size during the year as new 5-year-olds were taken in at the start of spring and summer terms. In order to examine the effect of class size on the three progress groups we looked at children who were in small classes (that is less than twenty pupils), children who were in classes of between twenty and thirty children, and those that were in classes of more than thirty. In fact only one class had more than thirty children in it. One hundred and thirty-five children were in classes of less

Table 4.6 Distribution of poor, average and good progress according to gender of children in the class

	Girls(%)	Boys(%)
Making least progress	34	37
Making average progress	33	32
Making most progress	33	31
Total	100	100

Table 4.7 Distribution of poor, average and good progress according to number of children in the class

Classes	Less than 20(%)	20–30(%)	More than 30(%)
Making least progress	32	40	26
Making average progress	30	33	39
Making most progress	38	27	35
Total	100	100	100

than twenty and 176 were in classes of between twenty and thirty. As can be seen from Table 4.7, again there was very little difference between how children had done in the different class sizes. With only one large class no conclusions can be drawn. Looking at Table 4.7 we can see that, although children in the smaller classes made more progress than those in average size classes, the largest class seemed to do as well or better than the smallest classes. Class size, therefore, does not seem to offer an adequate reason for the variations we have found.

Did the number of year groups in the class make any difference?

In the twenty classes in our sample there were classes that had two, three or four year groups. One of our criteria for selection of schools was that they would be primary schools with less than 100 pupils. A school of this size, of necessity, has to place more than one year group in each class. Indeed, one of the reasons for the research was to examine how such schools fared with the NLS which is based on a framework of objectives which designates objectives for particular year groups in particular terms.

In order to consider whether the differences in our sample were related to the number of year groups in the class we undertook a similar analysis to the ones above. Only three classes had four year groups: Mrs Milne's and Mrs David's Key Stage 2 classes and Mrs Harman's class which had children from reception through to year 3. One hundred and twenty-two children were in classes with three year groups and 168 in classes with two year groups. As can be seen from Table 4.8, there is very little difference between children in classes with two or with three year groups in them. It does appear that children in classes with four year groups do less well. However, Mrs Harman's had four year groups and this was one of the classes in which children made most progress. Clearly, the number of year groups in the class does not account for the variation we found.

Table 4.8 shows that a greater percentage of children did not do well in the reading tests in the classes with four year groups. Conversely, a smaller

Table 4.8   Distribution of poor, average and good progress according to number of year groups in the class

	2 year groups in the class (%)	3 year groups in the class (%)	4 year groups in the class (%)
Making least progress	31	37	48
Making average progress	33	31	31
Making most progress	36	32	21
Total	100	100	100

percentage of children made above average gains over the eight months in these classes. Yet these differences are small and were not found to be statistically significant.

Did whether the child was in the oldest or youngest year group in a mixed age class make any difference?

We had also speculated that particular groups of children in mixed age classes might do less well. It seemed possible that the youngest in a class that could have children aged between 4 and 8, or 7 and 11 could be disadvantaged. Equally the oldest children in classes with a wide age span could do less well. Table 4.9 shows how the progress scores were distributed according to whether children were in the youngest (e.g. a year 4 child in a year 4, 5, 6 class), middle or oldest year groups.

Again, there is very little difference between progress of the different age groups and these differences could have arisen by chance. There is some indication that the younger age groups were more likely to make more progress but no real conclusions can be drawn from this.

Did the attainment at the start of the year make any difference?

Sainsbury *et al.* (1998) in their evaluation of the first cohort of the NLP report that the lowest attainers made less progress than other groups in their sample. We, therefore, decided to examine our data to see whether there was any difference between children of different levels of attainment. We grouped children into three ability groups according to their standardised scores on the October tests. Thus we had three groups of those whose scores fell into the lowest third of all October scores, those whose scores fell into the middle band and those whose scores fell into the group representing the highest scores.

Table 4.10 shows the distribution of scores according to this grouping. Although this table shows that those children who had the lowest scores in October had made most progress and those whose scores were highest in October did not do so well on the reading test, this conclusion has to be

Table 4.9 Distribution of poor, average and good progress according to age position in the class

	Youngest year group in class (%)	Middle year group in class (%)	Oldest year group in class (%)
Making least progress	30	40	36
Making average progress	27	34	34
Making most progress	43	26	30
Total	100	100	100

Table 4.10 Distribution of poor, average and good progress according to child's score in October

Children	Lowest scores in October (%)	Average scores in October (%)	Highest scores in October (%)
Making least progress	22	32	54
Making average progress	38	35	23
Making most progress	40	33	23
Total	100	100	100

looked at with caution. It could be that this is a simple result of regression to the mean in which high and low scores from one test will become nearer to the average score when the test is repeated.

Were any of these findings statistically significant?

For all the tables above in which we had considered possible reasons for the differences in the amount of progress made by individual children we used chi-square to calculate the likelihood of the differences that we found arising by chance. Only the last set of statistics was found to be statistically significant at less than 5 per cent. That is for all but the last there was a stronger than 5 per cent chance that the differences were purely a result of chance differences. Indeed, although 5 per cent is the generally accepted level of significance, our level was a good way higher than 5 per cent indicating that there was every possibility that the differences were not attributable to the factors we tested for. Even though the last set of statistics, that of progress according to the child's October test score, was judged to be highly significant statistically it cannot be considered a good measure of differential progress as the differences are most likely to be a function of regression to the mean as explained above.

Thus we were left with the individual teacher being the only statistically significant factor that we have cognisance of that might account for the differences between children's progress.

What other reasons could there be for the differences?

There were, of course, other reasons that explain the differences we observed in the test results. Two of the schools had Ofsted inspection during the year, although this does not seem to have had a detrimental effect on progress. Two schools had the head teacher leave during the year. While one of these moves was a planned retirement, the other took place in a context of some anxiety. Although in the latter case the teachers showed evidence of stress in some of their interactions with children, there was no observable effect on their test results.

Other evidence of progress

Enjoyment of texts

One aspect of the life in literacy hour classrooms that was evident in almost all our sample was the enjoyment with which teachers and children used the enlarged texts for shared reading. In the interviews at the end of the first year, eight of the teachers specifically mentioned the shared reading and use of enlarged texts as a really positive feature of the literacy hour. Mrs Ibbotsen reflected the views of many at the end of the year when she said

> We are using the big books a lot more and I have found those to be very good and the children have really enjoyed them. . . . I have focused very much on the big books to keep the drip feeding of things like the author, the blurb and the way books are written, which I think is a key aspect for me anyway
>
> (Interview, June 1999)

Mrs Clark, another Key Stage 1 teacher, mentioned how her class got excited when they saw the new big book on the stand at the start of the week. Key Stage 2 teachers also found that their children enjoyed this aspect of the hour. Mrs David, although on the whole not positive about the literacy hour said 'I think they have enjoyed the big books, even the older children have enjoyed the big books. . . . It's still a novelty and they're very keen on the big books. So their interest has been good' (interview, June 1999).

Increased confidence

Sainsbury *et al.* (1998) in the NFER evaluation of the NLP included pupil attitude questionnaires in their study. They found that most children in their sample had positive attitudes to reading at the beginning and after 18 months of being taught through the literacy hour. The authors did not find any change in attitudes during this time. The most interesting finding arising from the pupil attitude questionnaire was the significant increase in children's confidence as readers.

The teachers in our study also felt that the literacy hour had improved children's confidence in themselves as readers.

The teaching of reading

Enjoyment and increased confidence cannot be the only reasons for the improvement shown in the national results. From our study of these classrooms there were evidently considerable changes made in how reading was taught:

- There was a reduction in the amount of time teachers spent reading with individuals, although some Key Stage 1 teachers continued to make time to hear readers or used other adults to do this.
- All classes implemented shared reading in some form.
- Most classes used some form of reading in groups, although few followed guided reading in the way envisaged by the NLS.

Shared reading

Shared reading gives children the chance to 'read' texts that they would not normally be able to read independently. The teacher, as the expert, reads a text that is beyond most children's ability to read on their own. Either by supplying the more difficult words, sustaining interest by use of intonation or enhancing comprehension through careful questioning, the teacher leads the less experienced reader into the world of texts at a level in advance of what they could do on their own. A typical example of this can be seen here, where Mrs Burns is working with a year 5/6 class on myths and legends. The text level objectives for the shared reading session are about the treatment of characters (minor heroes or villains) in myths and the use of narrative perspective (Y5,T2,T8). The extract below is from the second day of the week. On the Monday they had read a myth and identified main and minor characters. Today, Mrs Burns planned to read the story of *Thor's Wedding*, categorise the characters and talk about the perspective.

> Teacher reads aloud '*Thor's Wedding*' from OHP with a pointer while children follow. She reads with expression and great enthusiasm. . . . Teacher says it is an example of a story the Vikings would have told to each other, but points out this version has been modernised, using words like 'sexy'. Teacher asks whose perspective the story was told from and child answers it's a 'balance story'. (This must have been discussed before.) Teacher explains a lot of the story and relates bits that children can use in their own writing. Teacher explains how each character has a limited point of view and asks how the story would go if told, say, from the guard's point of view. Children involved and respond.
>
> (Field notes, January 1999)

Here we have many of the key features of the literacy hour and shared reading in particular:

- Children are 'reading' a text that is too hard for many of them to read on their own.
- They can see the text and are helped to follow the words by the 'expert'.
- The teacher models the behaviour of an experienced reader.

- The teacher draws children's attention to features of the text related to the objectives of the lesson.
- She draws on previous work.
- She shows children how the work can be related to their own writing.
- Children are involved in the session through engagement with the text and the teachers' questioning.

The children followed up the shared reading in independent work by writing brief versions of the story from the perspective of different characters. In the plenary, children from one of the groups read the first part of their versions of the story. The teacher asked whose perspective their version is told from, and how they showed their character in their writing. The observer wrote: 'teacher discusses, encourages to extend. Teacher compliments children's efforts and uses stories to illustrate points, i.e. how minor characters help to flesh out the story' (observation, January 1999). The observer also commented on how the class have become more 'involved, animated and confident in themselves' since the beginning of the year.

Guided reading

In the guided reading session, the teacher works with a group of children on a text of which they can read about 80 per cent on their own. The teacher guides children by providing some of the more unusual words in the text or directing them to identify the main theme of the text or key strategies that will help them understand. The idea being that this time is for children to be helped to gain independence as readers. An example of a guided reading session in key stage one is given below. Here Mrs Channing, the only teacher in the project who managed to hold two guided work groups within the 20-minute slot in the literacy hour on a regular basis, does guided reading with two groups from her reception/year one class (ages 4 to 6). In the example, you can see the difficulties she is having with this but also the potential for it to work effectively. Both notes from the observation schedule and the field notes are included to give a fuller picture. Each group is reading a different set of books from a published series. While she is with one group the other is doing a short spelling exercise. Meanwhile one reception group is playing a game based on *The Three Little Pigs* with the teaching assistant; another reception group is looking for other books with pigs in and making words with magnetic letters; the new reception children who have only been in school for three weeks are looking for 'f' words in a picture or making 'f' in the sand.

9.35: Spends some time explaining what to do so children will be independent so she can work with readers.

9.45: Teacher goes to second reading group. . . . Hands out *The Hungry Chickens* – asks children to look at cover picture and think why the chickens look sad. Turns to page 2 and points out print in speech bubbles and writing in a panel. Reads panel first, the children join in for speech bubble. Explains rhyming, picture clues. Teacher says only read to page 13. Then children are to read independently. Teacher listens and intervenes when needed.

9.52: Teacher says children must stop before last page and guess what the mother hen might say. Says must rhyme with 'patch'. Teacher prompts with 'What do chickens do?' i.e. scratch. Children read but find many words difficult, not using strategies they know and use regularly with the teacher.

(Observation, February 1999)

Teacher hears two groups in the guided reading at two different levels. First she makes comments on the book i.e. things to help them in their reading, then she tells them to read it out loud. She listens and intervenes when someone needs help. Inevitably she doesn't hear everyone's mistakes nor can she help everyone when they get stuck. She's looking for them to use strategies she uses with them to sound out or figure out new words when doing shared text work. However, they don't seem to be doing that (yet). Generally when someone is stuck s/he immediately looks up and listens to hear if someone else is at the same place and has the answer. If not s/he tends to skate over the word. With each group the teacher stops before they get to the last page and asks them to predict what will happen and what is the rhyming word? Teacher prompts and gives clues.

(Field notes, February 1999)

Although there were difficulties with this session as commented by the observer, eleven children were able to read aloud and received some teaching about how to read. There were several of the key features of guided reading evident here:

- The teacher was teaching children on texts that were the appropriate level for them to read mainly independently.
- She set up the classroom situation so as to avoid disturbance as much as possible.
- She supported children in their understanding of the text by setting the scene of the narrative.
- Children were encouraged to act independently.
- She encouraged them to use strategies that they had been taught and used regularly in shared work.
- She encouraged children to read for meaning as well as be concerned with decoding strategies.
- She encouraged them to think ahead in their reading.
- She highlighted the way a narrative works towards a conclusion that can be predicted from reading the text.

These experiences of shared and guided reading are very different from individual children reading to the teacher, which was the predominant way in which reading was taught before the NLS. In the literacy hour children and teachers do not have the chance to work as a pair talking about books. The child does not have the undivided attention of the teacher. The child is limited in the amount s/he can develop his/her own meanings in exploratory discussion with the teacher. The teacher cannot focus her teaching exclusively on the needs of just one child. Nevertheless, I would argue that these features were not always evident when teachers were sharing books with individuals. Pressure on teachers in large, busy classrooms meant that the reality was often quite different. Also giving the child the teacher's undivided attention when reading can make a child very dependent on the teacher for decoding unknown words.

The teachers in this project enjoyed the shared reading, but many found guided reading difficult. Over the two years they developed strategies that improved the management of these parts of the hour. Sometimes teachers found it easier to locate guided reading outside the hour while other children were reading independently or with parents at the start or end of the school day. This gave them more time to work on guided writing during the literacy hour. They also learned the importance of actively working to develop independence – it did not just happen. For example, they provided task cards (often with pictures for Key Stage 1), word banks, lists of 'what to do when stuck', and so on.

Teachers also raised important points about the NLS and reading that they were only partway successful in addressing. There were serious concerns about the nature of the reading experience that children experienced and teachers found it hard to find time to put this right:

- Teachers were concerned that a lot of shared reading was done on extracts of text.
- They worried that too much time was spent pulling texts apart and not enough studying the whole.
- They found that focused objectives in shared reading, reduced the opportunities children have to explore their own meanings.
- Few found time to read texts aloud purely for pleasure, particularly at Key Stage 2. The idea of the class novel seemed to be all but dead.
- Teachers regretted losing the joy of reading for its own sake.

Although after two years some had gone some way to changing this, they still felt something had been lost. As the two years went on, teachers began to introduce or reintroduce initiatives to encourage other opportunities to read and explore texts such as quiet reading, paired reading with older/younger partners, keeping book reviews/reading journals, doing drama related to texts, book making. However, there was no evidence of an increase in the amount of 'story time'.

Summary

The analysis of progress in reading made by children in the project according to the reading tests showed that there was considerable variation between the classes we tested. Although we tested for various factors that might have caused this difference the only one that showed any significance was the classteacher. Teachers, on the whole, enjoyed the shared reading and using big books but they found guided reading difficult to manage. They thought that children enjoyed the literacy hour but expressed concern that their experience of reading could become limited to reading and analysing extracts of text, particularly at Key Stage 2.

Advice for teachers

The increased focus on the teaching of reading that is an essential feature of the NLS has clearly been a successful element of the literacy hour. Giving all children access to good quality and challenging texts seems to have worked well. Using guided reading to help children learn to become independent readers, although difficult to manage, ensures that children's reading is monitored and that they get to read texts that are of an appropriate level for them. Evidence from observations of these teachers as they taught literacy hours and from what they said about their teaching points to the following advice:

- Remember the balance between shared and guided reading; where the teacher acts as expert and where the child is learning to become independent. The level of difficulty of the texts used, the purposes of the session and the role adopted by the teachers are different.
- Use good quality texts, chosen for their quality not just because they fit the objective.
- Involve all children in shared reading – less able readers will benefit from the enjoyment of good quality texts and hearing text read fluently.
- Use questions, prompts, highlights and so on to draw attention to features of the text.
- Model how readers behave when they are reading and also how readers think when they are reading. 'I wonder why he did that' or, 'I wonder what will happen next' show inexperienced readers how experts think while they are reading.
- Emphasise the links between reading and writing.
- Shared and guided reading give you the chance to teach skills in the context of a piece of text rather than as an isolated exercise.
- As well as reading in the literacy hour, give children the chance to explore texts in more open-ended ways through exploratory discussion, drama, art, and so on.
- Make sure you find time to read good stories aloud. Children need to hear extended text and experience the joy of being lost in a good book. Don't let other pressures squeeze this out.

5 Learning to write in the literacy hour

Introduction

It was clear from our observations and anecdotal evidence from elsewhere in the country that writing did not receive as much attention in the first year of the NLS as reading. The literacy hour was seen by many as being mainly concerned with reading. This impression was confirmed by the Ofsted evaluation of the first year of the NLS where they found that writing was taught less frequently and less effectively.

> Teachers are generally much more confident in teaching reading than writing, and consequently have given more attention to the former. . . . Guided writing or shared writing took place in only a minority of lessons. Consequently, in most lessons the only writing that took place occurred during the group and independent work. Too much of this writing was low level at best, it consisted of the consolidation or revision of previously learned skills, or more usually an undemanding task involving little more than copying from a simple text or filling in gaps in a work sheet.
>
> (Ofsted, 1999: paras 82 and 83)

One comment made by some of our teachers at the end of the year was that they found that the aspects of writing they taught were not picked up by children in their free writing. Results from National Curriculum assessments in English confirmed the differential progress made in the two years since the implementation of the NLS in reading and writing at key stage two. It seemed that even where writing was being taught it was not always taken up by children in their own writing – even in high-status instances such as national tests. (For results of National Test in English 1996–2000, see Table 4.1, page 50.)

Scaffolding writing

The NLS encourages the scaffolding of learning through explicit teaching, modelling and supported writing. For example, a class might look at the portrayal of a character in a story they have read and examine what the author does to create pictures in the mind of the reader. This would involve considering the kinds of words chosen, how they are used in sentences and how the whole piece hangs together. They would discuss how effectively the character is portrayed and why they think this. The teacher would then lead the joint construction of a portrait of a character in shared writing, using the opportunity to model the process of the composition and how an author might think while composing. Only then would children be expected to have a go at writing their own character portrait. Guided writing could support this independent writing with groups of children who needed additional teaching or specific support in aspects of the writing.

We saw very little evidence of this process occurring in our classrooms in the first year of the NLS. We did see quite a lot of the sort of practice described by HMI in which the independent writing set could be described as 'holding activities designed to keep the pupils occupied rather than develop or consolidate their language skills. Typically, such work took the form of low-level work sheets, word searches, copying exercises . . . simple cloze exercises, and even colouring-in' (Ofsted, 1999: para 76).

It was significant that many of the teachers recognised that the way they felt they were expected to teach writing in the NLS was not satisfactory. Teachers felt there was not enough opportunity to write at length and that, often, children produced 'scrappy pieces of work' and did not get the chance to write from experience such as the follow-up to a trip. Three of the Key Stage 2 teachers said they found what had been taught in the literacy hour did not pass over into children's free writing. Mrs James complained, 'You can say 'yes I've taught them that' and then they come and do a piece of free writing or they're doing a piece of science work and that piece of English that you've taught them in the literacy hour is not being used' (interview, June 1999). Mrs Quick reflected this view in the interview at the end of the first year when she said,

Need to Make the link behind why writing

> I'm not totally convinced its coming through in the quality of the content of their work in the way I'd like to see it. I feel that their free writing has become more inhibited despite the fact that we've planned it in that they have a session on a Friday when we do sustained or extended writing. It's not coming through in quite the way that it used to.
>
> (Interview, June 1999)

These teachers were observed to teach both reading and writing. However, although they both modelled reading, using an enlarged text and reading along with the children, they were not observed to do shared writing. Mrs Quick was only observed to do guided writing once during our visits; on most visits she was doing guided reading; nor did guided writing figure often in her plans. Mrs James did not do guided work during the hour, she set tasks for the class and then circulated and interacted with individuals.

The whole class sessions in which writing was taught were remarkably similar in the two classes. An objective from the Framework of Objectives was taken as the focus and teacher and children brainstormed ideas about the content of the writing. This resulted in a list of ideas written up on a white board or flip chart. These ideas were then used as a plan or scaffold for children's independent writing. These lessons were similar in format to some of the Key Stage 2 lessons shown on the early NLS training videos. A lesson of this type was observed one Friday in February. Mrs Quick was teaching about fables related to an enlarged version of the Aesop's fable *The Boy Who Cried Wolf* that they had read earlier in the week.

> 11.11: Teacher refers to moral: 'If you play tricks too often you won't be believed.' Teacher asks children to think of how to transfer this to school situations. Teacher paints a picture of someone giving a false fire alarm and what would happen. Teacher asks for children to help her set the scene for writing. Teacher writes [children's suggestions for] elements of a fable [based on a false fire alarm] on flip chart. Teacher obviously wants particular answers to her questions. Teacher enthusiastic. Children mostly responsive but some inattentive.

> 11.18: Have listed nine things that could happen in their fable. Teacher refers to 'Wolf Wolf' text as a model. Children quite excited. Teacher says they are going to write their own stories on same model. They must not use fire or wolf themes. . . . Children must make plans before they write their stories. They have half an hour to write. Plenary will be one chosen story.

> (Observation, February 1999)

In this literacy hour the task was an interesting one which seemed to motivate the class and it arose naturally from the reading that had been done earlier in the week. However, the plans for earlier in the week show no other input that might have provided tools for the writing task. Writing objectives were related to nouns, suffixes and antonyms. Moreover, there was no shared writing in which the teacher modelled the writing process itself. She wrote in front of the class in response to children's answers to her questions about the content of the piece, often appearing to have an already conceived response that she sought. This is quite different from modelling the process of composition in which the teacher shows how the elements of language that have been taught fit into the type of writing being composed. Both the teachers quoted above as being concerned that what they taught did not show up in children's writing, taught writing in this way, focusing on generating ideas about content with much less focus on language use. This is not to say that content is unimportant. Writers need to have something to write about but inexperienced writers also need help in how to say it.

When we looked at the description of literacy hours we had observed in classes where children had made progress in writing we found examples of shared writing in which the teacher modelled the process of composition itself. We also found that these teachers were more likely to teach and model the writer's use of particular aspects of language.

Progress in writing

So that we could judge the progress made by children in their writing we first of all brainstormed what might be the features of progress. We tried to avoid selecting only those features that are easily recognisable but tend to be more the secretarial or surface elements. Whilst these are important, we also felt that the child's personal voice should be encouraged to develop. We were mindful of the oft-quoted statement in the Cox report, 'The best writing is vigorous, committed, honest and interesting. We have not included these qualities in our statements of attainment because they cannot be mapped on to levels' (DES, 1988: 17.31). Therefore, the child's engagement in the writing and a sense of creativity was also sought even though we recognised it would not always be readily identifiable.

Having produced a list of aspects of writing that we felt would show progress, we took a sample of the pieces of writing from each year group and put them in some sort of impressionistic order. We then discussed our opinions and differences. Finally, we returned to our list and refined it. Thus, progress in writing was judged according to the following criteria (no hierarchy is implied in the order here):

* *Handwriting* to include legibility, correctness of letter formation and whether script was joined or print.
* *Spelling* to include phonic knowledge, number of words spelled correctly, use of spelling rules and correct spelling of homophones.
* *Punctuation* to include knowledge of punctuation marks and correct usage.
* *Vocabulary* to include range, quality and figurative use.
* *Sentence structure* including use of simple, compound and complex sentences, and range of connectives used.
* *Personal voice* as evidenced by individual style, originality and engagement with the topic.
* *Use of Standard English.*

We then judged each individual target child as to whether he or she had made progress in writing. We did this separately and then discussed and reconciled any differences. Although this process was not unproblematic we found a fair degree of agreement overall as to which children had made progress.

Teaching writing

Seven teachers appeared to us to be successful at teaching writing. We judged this by looking at the samples of writing we collected from the target children. These seven teachers had, at least, two target children in a two or three year group class, or, at least, three in a four year group class who made good progress in writing. This is hardly a foolproof way of judging success as we could just have been lucky (or unlucky) in our choice of child but we felt happy with the outcome when we compared our judgement of writing progress with the practice that we had observed in the classrooms. The sample is also too small for us to be able to draw any clear conclusion as to the relationship between what these teachers did and progress that children made. However, we have found it useful to analyse more closely the practice of these teachers and compare it to those teachers whose children seemed to make little or no progress in writing.

Seven teachers were identified as being successful at teaching writing. There were five Key Stage 1 teachers: Mrs Andrews, Mrs Harman, Mrs Noakes, Mrs Channing and Mrs Ibbotsen. Our study seems to reflect national test results that showed little improvement in writing at Key Stage 2, in that the only two Key Stage 2 teachers in whose class the target children made good progress were Mrs York and Mr Leonard. It is difficult to identify any commonalities between these seven teachers except that they were all observed to teach writing. Although in the other classes children were given writing tasks, the shared and guided sessions we observed were usually focused on reading.

Shared writing in which the teacher actually modelled the process of composition was mentioned earlier as possibly contributing to the extent to which what was taught was taken up by children in their own writing. Five of the seven teachers who were successful in teaching writing did shared writing with their class during the year. We cannot judge how many times, but it was either observed during our visits or evident in the plans for the week of our visit. Mr Leonard and Mrs Noakes did not plan to model composition as such but both taught writing explicitly to their class and wrote in front of children regularly.

Guided writing took place in six of these seven classes regularly, both when we were observing them and it was included in their plans for other occasions. In fact, only eight of the teachers in the whole sample did guided writing regularly. Again, it was Mr Leonard who did not do guided writing. The relationship between guided writing and progress in writing seemed worth investigating further. Using chi-square we calculated whether the relationship between those teachers who did guided writing and those children who made good progress in writing was statistically significant. It was found to be so at less than the 1 per cent level. This can be seen in Table 5.1.

Five of these seven teachers had a session for extended writing during the week. Only two of the Key Stage 1 teachers, Mrs Ibbotsen and Mrs

Table 5.1   Distribution of good and little progress in writing according to who did guided writing

	Progress in writing		
Guided writing	*Good progress*	*Little progress*	*Total*
Teacher did guided writing	15	5	20
Teacher did not do guided writing	10	21	31
Total	25	26	51

Channing did not. In fact of the twenty teachers, ten had a regular slot for extended writing sometime in the week. Most of these were added at some point during the year in response to their concern about lack of time for children to write at length.

Case study 1 – Heidi

Heidi was 5½ years old at the start of the year. She was in Mrs Andrews's class, which was a small class of fifteen year 1 and 2 children at the start of the year. Another nine year 1 children joined the class in January. Heidi was anxious about writing at the beginning of the year and needed encouragement to have a go. She needed help identifying initial sounds, was unsure of how to group letters into words and her understanding of sentence structure was weak. In the first week of September she wrote unaided this piece about herself:

> mays Heidi I ay5yer o-

During the year Heidi wrote mainly narrative from texts read in class but also wrote from personal experience and a letter to Father Christmas. Although her reading score changed little, showing an increase of only 1 point, her writing developed well. She learned to spell many common words correctly and make good phonetic attempts at others, e.g. *sked* for scared and *masv* for massive. Her letter formation, which was quite correct at the start of the year, remained good and her print script became neat with correct use of ascenders and descenders. Her use of vocabulary was varied and interesting. By July she was using full stops correctly to mark the end of sentences. Her writing showed a developing personal voice and she could write for an extended length of time and used complex sentences with an increasing range of connectives. In July she could write a page of writing, as can be seen from this extract from her account of a visit to the country.

> and in the cave it was pech black. and in the cave there
> was a conv [cavern] and I got sked when it was pech
> blcak. and when the conv came up. there was a rock. and I
> got sked and I neley trod on a tadpol but I did't like it. and
> at the End there was a watr fol and Jade's mum had to
> hlap us. and then we climbed up a hill

Mrs Andrews

Heidi's class teacher was Mrs Andrews. She had been teaching for many
years most of which had been in small schools. At the start of the year she
was uncertain about the literacy hour, worrying about the increased pace
with which things were to be covered. She was particularly concerned
about the least able and most able as she felt she would have to teach to
the middle range. Interestingly, she was also concerned that the focus
would be heavily on reading and therefore writing might be neglected. Her
teaching before the introduction of the literacy hour had been mainly using
an integrated day, in which children worked in groups on different aspects
of the curriculum. She did some whole class and group teaching. She had
already begun to reduce the amount of time she spent hearing children
read as the school had recently introduced group reading and this was
going well.

The inspection report for the school from September 1997 found
standards in English to be in line with national expectations and progress
to be satisfactory. The school themselves, following a year working on
developing reading, had identified writing as needing development.

With this background in mind it is interesting to consider the way in
which Mrs Andrews's teaching of the literacy hour developed over the year.
In the first term, each week seemed to follow a similar pattern of having a
key text, which the class read together on Monday, Tuesday and
Wednesday. On Thursday, they did shared planning of writing based on the
text and on Friday worked together as a class jointly constructing a class
version. A guided writing session in addition to the guided reading one was
introduced from December. In January the pattern of the week changed to
include extended writing instead of the literacy hour on Fridays. Mrs
Andrews continued to do both guided reading and guided writing in the
literacy hour. From February the pattern developed further. It became
established that the key focus for the week would be drawn to the class's
attention in shared reading and then Mrs Andrews would introduce the
writing task to groups in guided writing. For example, in March they were
working on the setting of stories using traditional tales. In guided writing
they started work on their own stories in which they were the central
character in a setting similar to the story read in shared reading. These

stories were continued during the other days in the week. The most able writers did guided writing on Tuesday, which gave them more time to develop their writing during the week. The least able writers did guided writing on a Thursday and wrote a sentence describing the giant's house following the reading of *Jack and the Beanstalk*. In extended writing on the Friday, they were asked to write a story set in the same setting as that of *The Princess and the Pea*.

Text level

As the year progressed, the focus of the guided writing changed. In the early sessions, Mrs Andrews would discuss the composition of the sentence and then write it on the flip chart with the children focusing on the spelling of individual words. Over the year this changed with the focus shifting from a focus on the spelling to more concern for the linguistic features and the best way to express their ideas. For example, in May, the class was looking at books written by Ruth Brown. On the observation visit the group was writing their own version of *The Dark, Dark, Tale*.

> 11.30 Teacher has written date and title on flip chart for children to copy. Teacher asks children how the story started, i.e. 'Once upon a time' and writes this. Teacher asks for places that are dark and writes suggestions at the bottom of the page e.g. train, tunnel, school, castle, shed, drawer, box, cupboard, cave hole, dungeon. Children responsive, teacher validates suggestions, then encourages children to write their own story. Emphasises Ruth Brown's use of position words to start the sentences e.g. 'above', 'on', 'at the front of', and use of 'dark, dark'.
>
> (Observation, May 1999)

Word level

From looking at her plans and the evidence of our observations, Mrs Andrews usually followed the same pattern for word-level work. She did not use the Framework of Objectives but would take letters or groups of letters, representing single phonemes or clusters, work on them individually each day and then revise the group. For example, in the week beginning 11 January she taught 'ai' on Monday, 'ae' on Tuesday, 'ay' on Wednesday and reviewed the three ways of writing the long a vowel phoneme on Thursday. She did the same sort of thing in other weeks with 'oo', end consonant clusters, 'are' and so on. This enabled her, over one year, to cover most of the phonic objectives for the two year groups in her class. She felt this was important as the pace was much faster in the NLS than they had previously adopted with these children. From February she noted a separate objective for a small subset of the class.

Lessons followed a similar pattern throughout the year, although she shifted from making words with magnetic letters in the first term to writing em on the white board from January. She would ask for words containing the relevant grapheme and then write each of these on the white board eliciting spelling from the children as she wrote. She would create lists, emphasising the pattern of similar spellings. When a child suggested a word with a different spelling she would write it elsewhere on the whiteboard.

Independent work

Activities that children did during the independent time varied. Usually one group had a spelling activity, which might include collecting words and making them into sentences or a worksheet. Sometimes children played with magnetic letters or listened to story tapes. Sentence writing activities included writing the last line of a limerick, writing an alliterative sentence and writing information found in a book. Groups with a teaching assistant made up a group story on one occasion and on another did some role-play based on the shared text.

At the end of the year

At the end of the year, Mrs Andrews said she was surprised how well the literacy hour had gone. She felt her practice had changed considerably in that her work, particularly phonic work was much more structured and she had covered much more ground, both because of the pace of progression and because she was aware of a much wider range of objectives. She found she did much more whole class teaching and was much more aware of her objectives. She felt that she now challenged children more and in a much more focused way. She still had her same concerns about supporting the underachievers and challenging the most able. She still felt that there was not enough opportunity for children to write at length, which was why they had introduced extended writing one day each week.

When we revisited Mrs Andrews's class at the end of the following year, they had done well in the national tests for writing. For two years they had now had no children who were Level 1 in writing, and, in 2000, they had two-thirds of the class at 2b or above, as opposed to half in the two previous years. However, they still had no children who achieved Level 3. Mrs Andrews continued to do shared writing at least once a week and guided writing four times a week with extended writing on the fifth day. Despite this she said she regretted the reduced opportunities for children to write at length and found the guided writing the most difficult part of the literacy hour because of constraints of time. She felt that children did not always have enough time to develop their skills.

If I try to isolate the features of Mrs Andrews's practice that may have contributed to the success of the target children in her class in writing, I would suggest the following points:

- Clear links between the work in reading and the work in writing.
- Explicit teaching of writing focusing on the use of language as well as the content and form.
- Children seeing the teacher write, whether in response to what they have said or from her own composition.
- Extensive use of praise for children's contributions.
- High expectations of the level of work they will be able to achieve.

Case study 2 – Rachel

Rachel, in year 5, was 9 years and 9 months at the start of the year. She was in a class of thirty-two children, from years 4, 5 and 6. Her writing samples show she undertook a range of writing during the year. Mostly the writing was fiction and imaginative but how these came about varied. For example, she wrote an extract from Mr Tom's diary from the book *Goodnight Mr Tom* by Michelle Magorian, used planning sheets, wrote a first person account of an incident, responded to a letter of complaint. Most of the pieces are short but we know that Mr Leonard reintroduced extended writing during the year.

In September her spelling showed poor knowledge of vowels digraphs, although her errors were mostly phonetically regular, e.g. *montin, frezing, gess.* She also showed evidence of transitional spelling with *blet* for belt and *fourntly* for fortunately, *thourgh* for threw. She also showed poor graphic knowledge, making regular mistakes with inflected endings, e.g. *carryed* and adding apostrophe 's' for plurals. By the end of the year her knowledge of vowel digraphs had improved and she had few spelling mistakes (and these are good phonetic attempts, e.g. *pittafull*). However, she had still not learned to form plurals. She still used homophones, e.g. *caught* for court.

Full stops and capital letters were in place at the beginning of the year and she used commas from December. She also used a range of other punctuation marks such as exclamation marks, and dots such as. . . . She was using complex sentences from the beginning of the year but towards the end her usage was more literary; for example, when she wrote, 'As they pulled out the dead body of Deadlock form the lake they stood around looking at him with pittafull sadness'.

Mr Leonard made frequent use of writing frames and their influence can be seen in, for example, her letter to someone who (supposedly) had complained about her class misbehaving on a school trip (see Figure 5.1).

Mr Leonard frequently focused on children's use of vocabulary and this is reflected in Rachel's writing. Her vocabulary is imaginative and interesting and she makes good use of adjectives and adverbs. This can be seen in her writing of 'The Final Chapter' (see Figure 5.2).

Despite the obvious influence of the teacher in her writing, her own personal voice is not lost. This can be seen in the way she engages with the

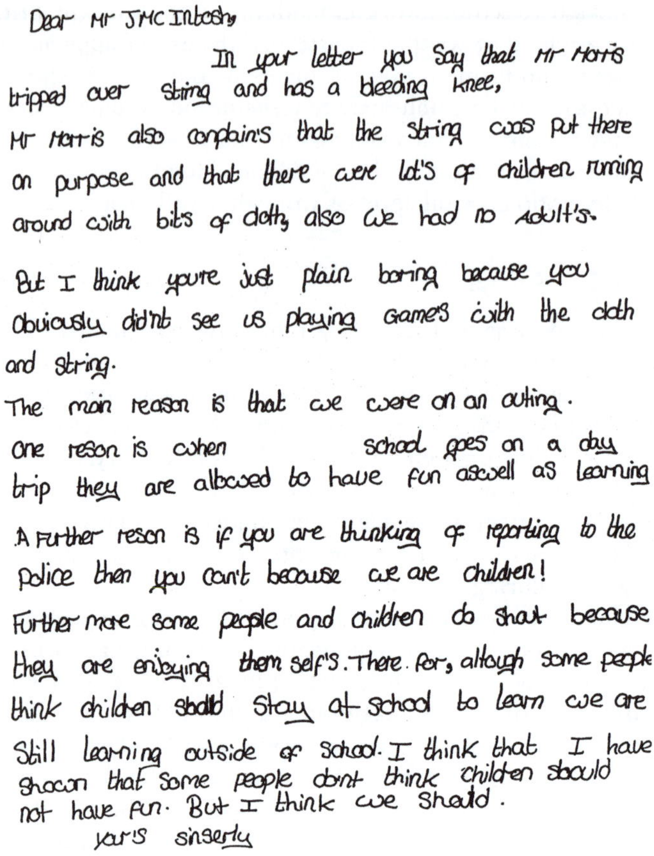

Dear Mr JMC Intosh,

In your letter you say that Mr Morris tripped over string and has a bleeding knee, Mr Morris also complains that the string was put there on purpose and that there were lot's of children running around with bits of cloth, also we had no adult's.

But I think you're just plain boring because you obviously did'nt see us playing Games with the cloth and string.
The main reason is that we were on an outing.
One reson is when school goes on a day trip they are allowed to have fun aswell as learning
A Further reson is if you are thinking of reporting to the police then you can't because we are children!
Further more some people and children do that because they are enjoying them self's. There for, although some people think children should stay at school to learn we are still learning outside of school. I think that I have shown that some people dont think children should not have fun. But I think we should.
yor's sinserly

Figure 5.1   Rachel, aged 10 years, showing influence of writing frame.

different writing tasks. For example, in her first-person account of an adventure in a rainforest she wrote 'Now, I am master of designs but today it all went wrong, they saw me and that's bad' (March 1999). In her Data File on a monster, she wrote 'If you get in the way of this thing you do'nt see light again, He's got a big appertite. What to do if you meet him on a dark night. . . . Do not fight him just RUN!!?' (July 1999).

Mr Leonard

Mr Leonard presents an interesting case study in the search to find what might be the contributory factors to the successful teaching of writing. He was one of only two Key Stage 2 teachers who we identified as having children who made good progress in writing. Mrs York's class also seemed to make good progress but we will describe her practice elsewhere (see

Chapter 7). Mr Leonard, although mainly positive about the literacy hour never really adopted it completely. He had a flexible approach from the beginning and would often move elements of the hour to different times and was not afraid to set non-literacy tasks in independent work. He was never observed to do guided work, preferring to set tasks and then move around the class interacting with individuals. He also introduced his own objectives alongside ones taken from the NLS. However, a clear pattern to his teaching of writing can be identified.

Features of his teaching of writing are:

- The fact that he would identify a type of writing that the class would be working on.
- How he drew attention to the features of that writing from enlarged texts in shared reading.
- That he gave children the chance to have a go at trying the type of writing.
- He clearly identified what made a good piece of writing.
- That he used writing frames frequently to illustrate features of text or to help some children in their composition.
- That he would use an example of a child's work in the literacy hour and consider ways in which it might be improved, encouraging children to respond with their own opinions but also giving his own.
- He set individual targets for children to improve their writing.

We did not observe any examples of the joint construction of text in which the composition of a piece of writing was modelled but we did see several occasions when he modelled the redrafting of an existing piece of writing.

An example of a typical series of lessons in Mr Leonard's class is the following, which took place in June 1999. The text type was stories with unfamiliar settings and the learning objectives related to drafting and redrafting and the use of adjectives. By this time in the year he had adopted the practice of planning his week with four quasi literacy hours and a fifth day which was used for extended writing. Early in the week the shared text was *Nheena and the Udorn Tree* with which, amongst other things, they had looked at the use of adjectives. On the day of our observation visit they were looking at some selected pieces of writing that the class had done in the previous week on *Tarka the Otter* (Williamson). He starts by reviewing work they have already done on redrafting and runs through the format, which they appear to know well. The following are extracts from the field notes, which give a good idea of the format of the lesson.

Teacher has drafting redrafting summary on an OHT to discuss points. Children read out the points and teacher questions or elaborates. He reminds them that they've talked about these before and there's nothing new. Teacher then puts a piece of child's writing on OHP to talk about. Everyone reads the first sentence and teacher asks what they like about it. Asks what makes this a good sentence but teacher emphasises his own opinion. Teacher and children discuss power words e.g. 'shrill', 'retreated'.

(Field notes, June 1999)

The children then get into pairs and look at examples of another child's work that has been redrafted. They are given a copy of the notes on redrafting and are asked to comment on how well the writer has addressed the points. The teacher goes around encouraging children to think about the task. They have 10 minutes for this. On their return to the carpet the teacher asks for feedback on good use of words. Children contribute 'astonishment' and 'scornful'. The children then return to their tables to work on their own drafts.

Teacher goes to individual children to help them with their ideas. The class is quiet and focused. After 12 minutes the teacher tells children to put their hands up if they think they have used this time well. Reminds them that they must work faster. Teacher then conferences with individual children as they finish their work. Teacher seems intimately involved in children's work and progress. After 25 minutes, teacher stops children to tell them they have had 25 minutes for writing. He asks who's pleased with what they have done. Makes comments on progress. Teacher signals they have 10 minutes to finish now and have the responsibility to choose how best to use this time.

(Field notes, June 1999)

Rachel the year 5 target child from this class produced a piece of work from this series of lessons (see Figure 5.2).

The Final Chapter

As they pulled out the dead body of Deadlock from the lake they stood around looking at him with pittafull sadness. The hunter's looked back at the lake and saw a bubble rise and then burst, then another rose and broke and finally the third bubble did exactly the same. They walked back carrying the dead Deadlock on their shoulders, as they did they heard the mournful laughter of Tarka the Otter. Tarka swam painfully through the water, he then heard a familiar screeching voice coming from up ahead, as he swam nearer there waiting for him was his old mate White Tip. Tarka ran quickly towards her in astonishment, they then went back to the holt. Soon after there were four little cubs living with Tarka and White Tip in the holt.

And here ends the

Story of Tarka the Otter

(Rachel, year 5, 7 June 1999)

Figure 5.2   Rachel, aged 10 years, *The Final Chapter*.

It is interesting to examine this series of lessons to see those elements of the NLS that the teacher has incorporated into his teaching and where he has retained his previous practice. In the end of year interview Mr Leonard said that he felt he had a 'proper scheme of work for English now' and that the NLS had raised his expectations of what children could achieve. He felt he did more direct teaching and longer whole class sessions than before and had increased the pace of his lessons. He also felt he had learned to use the objectives more effectively by having less each week so he could really work at something. He mentioned few negative points (which is hardly surprising since he had adapted the hour to suit his teaching). One point he did mention was that he found a kind of monotony of doing the same pattern each day.

Two years after the introduction of the NLS he was still following the same sort of format with an adapted literacy hour on four days a week and extended writing on the fifth. He still felt the objectives were helpful but was still adapting those from the framework to fit his needs. He admitted he was now more likely to abandon the literacy hour for some blocks of work and felt more confident to be flexible about how he managed his literacy teaching. He altered what he did to some extent in that, instead of just moving around individuals during the independent work, he focused on working mainly with one group while still making sure he had seen what each child in the class was doing. He said he felt happier about children's performance in reading than in writing but did think that there was some improvement in that children now had a much clearer idea of what a good piece of writing was like and how to structure their writing. Like Mrs Andrews, he regretted the lack of time for children writing at length, although this happened at least once a week in his class. He also said he found it hard to keep the quality of the work when children were working independently. He did feel that what he had taught could be observed in children's free writing, some of the time. He found this worked well when children had a specific target to focus on. He also described a poetry writing block of work that had culminated in the class writing sensory poems following a trip out in which they had lain in the grass and experienced the atmosphere. He had been pleased to notice that some children in their poem had drawn on the work they had done in the literacy hour on personification.

Both of these teachers described the way in which, as well as doing most of their teaching from the Framework of Objectives, they also developed objectives from their assessment of the needs of individual children. In both schools, target setting for individual pupils had been well established for the two years that we visited the schools. It also seems significant that both schools were active in a range of literacy initiatives. They both belonged to a group of small schools working to improve boys' performance in literacy and provided other literacy based experiences for the classes such as a visiting author and mentoring projects where young and older children were paired for literacy work.

Unhelpful practice

Another aspect of teacher behaviour that may have contributed to the difference in progress in writing in the different classes was the way in which some teachers were reluctant to give up practices that they had used in the past. Don, a 5-year-old, year 1 child at the start of the project, was in a class whose pupils made good overall progress in reading. However, his writing experience did not match up to the expectations of the literacy hour. First, Mrs Clark, his teacher, did not let him write independently: he was always given the spelling of words he did not know. In September, with the help of a classroom assistant he wrote:

> At the weekend I wet to buy A new carpet it was gold and blue.

In contrast to the variety of writing experience in other classes, Don's teacher decided to retain the previous practice of children writing their news each Monday morning; he also wrote some stories. In the independent time children were given worksheets or copying tasks. When they had to do sentence writing they were given particular words to use and had to ask the teaching assistant for spelling. Thus, they had no opportunity to experiment with spelling, and little chance to explore vocabulary choice and composition. Don's reading score increased by 12 points but his writing showed far less development. At the start of the year his letter formation was inaccurate and this did not improve, although it was even and written on lines. He learned to use full stops. He increased the length of his writing but continued to use mainly simple or compound sentences joined by 'and' and 'then'. As the demands made on his written expression were very similar, his writing tended to follow the same pattern of his first piece. His vocabulary was unadventurous although by the end of the year he had begun to use adjectives to add interest to his writing. At the end of June, he was asked to write a story about a 'Secret Garden', with the support of the teacher who provided spellings:

> Once upon a time there was a secret house I went in the house and I found the rusty key I opened the creaky door. There was a beautiful Garden. It had a fountain and a pond and I saw bluebells.

Here, although the length has increased and the vocabulary is more interesting, there is little sense of narrative and the language itself follows the same formula as all the rest of his pieces.

At the end of the second year, Mrs Clark still liked the structure of the NLS and said that the children loved the work on big books. However, she said that the children's writing had not improved, even though this had been a focus in the school for 18 months. She said she was finding it hard to develop imagination with such a structured scheme. She found 20 minutes was too short for young children to write and was continuing to do news as a writing activity on the fifth day. In this case also it does seem that what teachers put into the literacy hour is reflected in children's progress. This teacher worked enthusiastically and in a focused way with big books and the children enjoyed and made progress in reading. Although she worked hard giving children the opportunities to write and did many spelling activities, she did not plan to develop children's composition or confidence as writers. As with some other teachers there was a sense that she expected the literacy hour to do it for them.

Summary

The teaching of writing in the literacy hour was not as successful in the first two years as the teaching of reading both in the classes in our project and from evidence from national test results. Writing within the NLS should be:

- linked with reading,
- scaffolded by the teacher using demonstration, modelling, frames, etc.,
- planned to link shared to guided to independent writing,
- planned with teaching objectives related to language use as well as content.

The teachers in our study whose children seemed to make good progress in writing seemed to feature the following elements in their teaching:

- They linked reading and writing within the week.
- They drew attention to features of text.
- They regularly wrote in front of children.
- They made it clear what a good piece of writing entailed.
- They gave children the opportunities to write different kinds of writing.
- They focused on the use of language as well as the content.
- They planned to develop aspects of composition, e.g. drafting, imagination, interesting vocabulary.
- They planned their teaching from assessment of groups and individuals as well as the Framework.
- They provided a range of literacy experiences beyond the hour.

Advice for teachers

Although there are no clear links between a set of teaching strategies and good progress in writing, it is possible to suggest ways in which teachers might use the structure of the NLS to develop writing:

- A progression of work from reading a text or text type to writing developed from this, is likely to help children understand the relationship between the two sides of literacy.
- Drawing attention to features of text and considering what impact they have makes explicit for children what might otherwise go unnoticed.
- Teachers can demonstrate and model how writers write and how writers think as they write. Perhaps in the past some children have not gained an understanding of what writers actually go through as they write.
- Planning to work on aspects of language use as well as helping children think of the content may help children develop a broader repertoire of writing styles.
- The Framework of Objectives provides a structure and set of teaching objectives but this should not stop teachers evaluating and teaching to the needs of the class, and groups or individuals within the class. Some children, especially boys, appreciate having clear targets to work on.
- Children should have experience of reading and writing a range of different types of texts. They need to have the chance to explore the composition of written language in a whole range of ways: oral and written; short and long; prescribed and open.
- Twenty minute slots do not mean that children cannot develop longer pieces of writing. The teachers in our study gave children the chance to develop pieces over several days, working on planning, drafting, revising, and editing. Children also wrote for longer periods of time on some days. Children wrote for work in other curriculum areas.

6 Changing practice at Key Stage 1

Introduction

All ten schools in the project were different. They differed in size, in how they taught literacy before the introduction of the NLS, in type of environment and in teachers' attitudes to the NLS. Having said this, however, they do give a fairly representative picture of classroom practice both before and after the introduction of the NLS.

I have chosen to describe the Key Stage 1 class at Hawthorne Primary School because I feel it represents a class in which children made fair to good progress over the first year of the implementation of the NLS. As I explained earlier, there was no clear distinction between classes that did really well and classes that did really badly. Overall, children made slightly more progress according to reading tests scores than might have been expected but there were large variations in average progress scores between classes. The picture was the same with writing: some classes had children who made very little progress in writing whereas others had children who made good progress. Mrs Harman seems to me to represent a teacher who has made considerable changes in her way of working without losing her principles of what she considers good primary practice. And she has done this with some success.

Hawthorne Primary

Hawthorne Primary School is a small primary school situated in a rural village. The village has staggering hill-top views over a wide river valley. The small community of 350 is contained in 133 houses with a usual village spread of people including the elderly and a range of family types. The population is made up partly of farmers and other self-employed people and of commuters to surrounding towns. There is not a lot of money around and many people live in rented accommodation. Among the houses clustered on two roads is a pub/shop, a church and a village hall. Facilities for children are limited to a play park and there is a bus service that runs twice a day. Ofsted commented in their report that the children start at a lower level than expected at Hawthorne Primary School because of the economic make-up of the village.

There are just two classes in the school: Mrs Harman's class which, in the year of the project, had reception to year 3 and a Key Stage 2 class that had years 4, 5 and 6 children in the one class which was taught on most days by the head teacher.

Mrs Harman

Mrs Harman is an experienced teacher. After her initial training she taught in a small school for two years and then in a large school. After having a family she came back into supply teaching and then to a full-time post. At the time of the project she had been teaching at Hawthorne School for eight years.

On the Teachers' Beliefs about Literacy Questionnaire (TBALQ) she rated herself as midway between child-centred and structured. However, her rating according to her answers to the questions made her the most child-centred of all the teachers with the highest score of 94 (within a possible range of 24–120).

Before the introduction of the NLS she had planned her work around topics and texts. She would often follow a text for more than a week and base much of her literacy work on this text. She kept careful records of what children had done and favoured this to an objectives-led approach. She was concerned about how she would be able to plan her work according to objectives as required by the NLS.

> Last year and up to now, I hadn't done the formal planning in the way I was expected to do. It's been retrospective planning, 'What have I done and what have I got to . . .?' I think I like doing it in that way because you get a book and the book itself... . If it's a good text like *When the Door Bell Rang*, and you get so much out of it that it just comes to you and you haven't chosen that book because you want to do this, that or the other. I just don't work that way, I get inspired by what's happening in [the book].'
>
> (Interview, July 1998)

She described her approach to the teaching of reading as 'guided free choice' and used the Oxford Reading Tree as a basic reading scheme but allowed children choice of other texts as well. Children were encouraged to take books home when they wanted and could choose any book they liked. She also had a quiet reading time in the afternoon when children were allowed to browse through books. She taught phonics regularly, particularly to help with spelling but admitted it was mostly with the younger children for 'initial sounds and blends'.

She explained that her teaching of writing had developed in the year coming up to the NLS in that she was becoming aware of the need to get children to write in different genres. However, she remained keen to give children the choice of what they wrote so that, whereas she might model one form of writing, children could choose what they wanted to write. She explained,

> Well we've always had this sort of traditional Monday, that they do their own writing about whatever they want, or something that's happened at the weekend, and I start off by modelling mine on the white board. So we do it together and then I might pick out and talk about sentences or capital letters or I might miss a word and they know what's going to come next and we talk about that . . . and all sorts of things that come up.
>
> (Interview, July 1998)

In the previous year she had introduced cursive writing following attending a course given by Christopher Jarman but was unsure about how it was working. She said

> I write like that [joined style] but then when they are learning letters they obviously do it . . . I'm in two minds about that, about how to help them, how to insist on their writing from the word 'go' as joined up. I sort of do and I don't.
>
> (Interview, July 1998)

On the whole, Mrs Harman's attitude to the NLS was mainly positive but she worried about the work being separated from other curriculum areas. She was unsure about how she could reconcile her very responsive, child-centred approach with the structure and planning requirements of the NLS.

Attainment in reading

Mrs Harman's class was one of the Key Stage 1 classes in which the children showed quite large increases in their reading test scores. At the start of the year they had had the second lowest average of all classes and the lowest Key Stage 1 average with a class mean of 97 as compared to the sample mean of 101. Standardised scores ranged from 85 to 118 with only five children having a score of more than 100. By June the class average had gone up to 104 as compared to 102 which was the sample mean in June. Standardised scores ranged from 90 to 128 and now thirteen children had a standardised score of more than 100. All but two children had made some increase in standardised score and those who had not had only changed by 2 or 3 points – an insignificant difference which could be attributed to differences in conditions on the day of the test. The class mean was now the ninth highest of the sample and the class ranked third of all classes in terms of progress.

Attainment in writing

As we have seen in the earlier chapters, the reading test scores, while interesting, by no means gave an unequivocal measure of progress. Evidence from target children's writing samples was another informative means of judging progress. The monthly samples from Mrs Harman's class showed children continuing to write news but also about their personal feelings, narrative and writing from a class text.

Jack, a year 1 child learned to write with a confident hand and to form his letters correctly. He used emergent writing and by the end of the year could spell a good range of words phonetically and used the correct spelling of many simple words. By the end of June he was using full stops. He used an interesting range of vocabulary such as 'telescopic arm' when writing about farm machinery. He used mostly compound sentences joined by 'and' but was also using some complex sentences with 'when' and 'because'.

Keith, in year 2, increased the length of what he wrote over the year and he learned to do a joined script. By March, he was using full stops and capital letters when reminded about them, but he did not use them consistently. Mrs Harman had emphasised the importance of phonics in spelling and Keith's spelling depended heavily on phonemic strategies. At the beginning of the year his spelling was largely phonemic, for example, *shud* for should, *pepul* for people, *sucul* for school, *finisht* for finished. By April, he could spell a wider range of words correctly, such as, would, please, when, were, loud, waiting, dinner, carrots but still relied on phonemic strategies as, for example, in *headfons* for headphones. He also showed signs of developing morphological strategies as in his spelling of *changeing* for changing and using his visual memory as in *frenids* for friends. Although he mostly used compound or simple sentences he was learning to use complex sentences in his writing, in the use of when, or after that, in chronological writing.

Although his writing is no more than National Curriculum Level 2, he does show an enthusiasm when he is writing about something in which he is interested. In January he wrote about a cold day 'We went to the trough and we looked in it. There were ice, ice and more ice . . . and after that we started to find more. We looked in the bucket and there were more! Ice!' (25 January 1999 spelling and punctuation corrected).

Engagement

All the teachers in our study got on well with the children in their classes. Children were mostly happy and settled. Various occurrences during the year made some teachers more stressed than others but this did not cause either a breakdown of discipline or distress to the children in any of the classes. Indeed, many of the teachers were very talented at engaging children's interest and the classes were enthusiastic happy places to learn. A feature of both the observations and the field notes is the number of references to children's response: their enjoyment, involvement, eagerness to contribute, attentiveness and absorption. The target children in Mrs Harman's class in almost all the observations (4 points in every literacy hour) were observed to be either attentive or contributing. Their enthusiasm for their work was marked and they always seemed very keen to contribute.

Use of texts

Shared reading

Mrs Harman had described at the start of the year how she liked to work from texts and was enthusiastic about the use of big books. On our visits to her class during the year she was observed to use a good range of fiction or poetry texts: *Willy and Hugh* by Anthony Browne; *The Jolly Witch* by Dick King Smith; the traditional story of *The Princess and the Pea* (Collins fairytales); *Rockpool Rap* from the Oxford Reading Tree Rhyme and Analogy series; *Cats Sleep Anywhere* by Eleanor Farjeon; *Along Came Eric* by Gus Clarke; *The Three Wolves and the Big Bad Pig* by Trivizas; *Where's my Baby?* by Julie Ashworth and John Clark. She did not have a big book to use every time but always made sure that children could see an enlarged version of the part on which she was focusing, either by using an OHT or by an enlarged photocopy. In shared text work she would read through the text using a pointer and making sure that children could see clearly. A feature of this part of the hour with this class was children's enjoyment and involvement in the reading. A typical description from the observer's field notes gives a sense of the scene. The teacher introduced *The Three Little Wolves and the Big Bad Pig* by reading the blurb on the back and reviews from the newspaper:

> Teacher has an enlarged passage from the book on the bookstand, which she reads aloud using a pointer, having first checked to make sure everyone can see. She says this is the beginning of the story and it 'sets the scene'. When a kangaroo pushing a wheelbarrow is mentioned she asks why they aren't giggling as was predicted in the reviews. Teacher and children discuss making pictures in their heads versus looking at the illustrations to try to answer this one. Teacher asks questions about the different characters in the story. I think the Teacher had planned to use the enlarged passage more exclusively, but the children wanted her to read the whole book so she continued reading the story and showing the illustrations. Teacher reads with expression. By the end of the book the children were joining in on the refrain. . . . Otherwise, the children seemed absorbed in the story making only occasional comment.
>
> (Field notes, May 1999)

There is a sense in these sessions that the teacher is also enjoying the text. For example, she introduces a poem by saying it is one of her favourites and sometimes gives her own personal response to the text alongside the children's. The use of big books in shared reading is one aspect of the hour that Mrs Harman felt most positive about,

> using the big books . . . it's real books, good books by proper authors with lovely language and illustrations and I think that is one of the greatest aspects of the literacy hour – just an enthusiasm for the books to pass on a love of reading, I think.
>
> (Interview, July 1999)

Guided reading

Guided reading was not observed during the visits as Mrs Harman decided to do this each afternoon outside the literacy hour. She found it difficult to get to two guided groups during the 20-minute period and so decided to concentrate on guided writing during the hour and to do guided reading during a quiet reading time in the afternoon. As a small school they had had only a small amount of money to spend on resources and she found it difficult to resource guided reading with books at the appropriate levels. She found she had to repeat using some books, resorted to using books from previous National Curriculum tests and used poetry books quite a bit.

Questions

The use of questions is recognised as a feature of effective practice, although the nature of the questions is important. Wells (1987) argues that some questioning does no more than require the children to guess the mind of the teacher. Whereas Fisher (1995) points out that certain questions can help children's understanding to develop.

Mrs Harman used questions in a range of ways:

- To check on children's knowledge
  What letter comes after 't'?
- To check on children's understanding
  What does bedstead mean?
- To link with previous work
  How is this different from yesterday's poem?
  What other stories have wolves in them?
- To encourage prediction
  What do you think the next words will be? (repetitive text)
- To focus attention on particular features of the text
  What sort of person was Mrs Jolly? How do you know?
  What made you think the pig was bad?
  How do you know the witch isn't nasty?

- To encourage metacognition
  How do you know?
  What words tell you that?
- To encourage comparison of one text with another
  What do you notice in this story that is different from the version that we all know?
- To make links with writing
  How would you start this story?
- To encourage evaluation of the text
  Do you think that was a funny ending?

Questions were used to engage children and to encourage them to think about aspects of the text from meaning and response to individual words and letters. Questions can impede involvement by being what Wells (1987) describes as 'display questions', doing no more than requiring children to display what they know. Mrs Harman used questions to stimulate children's thinking and to draw attention to features. This was not a simple matter of guessing the answer to closed questions with the answers already fixed in the teacher's mind but a shared process of exploring text. On one occasion the observer writes 'Teacher then asks comprehension questions about the story so far and discusses the old fashioned words used in the story. . . . The teacher is happy to answer any questions and go through the text in a relaxed way' (field notes, January 1999).

Change to literacy teaching

With all the teachers we observed as part of the project and others we worked with in other capacities during the first year of implementation of the NLS, there were greater or lesser degrees of tension between their previous practice and what they perceived the NLS required them to do. Mrs Harman was one teacher who seemed to manage to steer a course between fulfilling the requirements of the NLS and retaining aspects of her practice that she had developed over the years of her experience. Indeed, to say 'steer a course' implies that this was a difficult process, it might be more accurate to describe the process as one of assimilation.

Focused teaching

As was described earlier in this chapter, Mrs Harman was the teacher who was identified as being most child-centred from the Teachers' Beliefs about Literacy Questionnaire administered at the start of the project. Before the NLS, she followed the possibilities offered by the texts she used and the response of the class to decide what to teach and when. She allowed children mainly free choice of the books they read at school and at home. She said, 'I used to spend much longer doing one thing, say story writing and we would all start off and all write a story. It might take all morning because they get into it . . .' (interview, July 1998). Clearly, teaching literacy in a structured literacy hour could cut across her previous practice of following the needs of the children as she perceived them, rather than following a prescribed framework. However, she seemed to manage to retain responsiveness to her class within a far more structured programme than she had used previously.

After two years she was still enthusiastic about the literacy strategy and said she could not remember how she taught before. She said that she felt her teaching was more varied, in that she covered more aspects of language. She also felt she was more focused. She mentioned particularly the teaching of phonics where she felt she had changed to teaching how to apply the skills rather than just knowledge of letters. A caveat to this was that she felt this could inhibit the youngest children in their emergent writing as they had become so good at working out plausible spellings. She was considering ways of redressing the balance in the following year.

Pace

Pace has been identified as an element of successful teaching both by the NLS documentation and the Effective Teachers of Literacy project (Medwell *et al.*, 1998). Although well-paced lessons at Key Stage 2 seemed important, we had some concerns about how effective this would be with the younger children. It became important to define what was meant by the term pace. It is clearly not a simple matter of rushing children through the work to fit the requirements of the hour. At key stage one we felt the term 'purposeful' matched the needs of the children better and described what teachers were doing in successful literacy hours.

Some teachers in our study allowed the clock to become the guiding force in the hour with comments such as 'We must stop now or we will run over', referring to the time. Mrs Harman kept to the time sections of the hour for the most part but was still able to be flexible when it seemed appropriate. For example, when reading the story of *The Jolly Witch* by Dick King Smith she spent longer on the text level work than planned. The observer wrote, 'They spend a good amount of time giving suggestions and considering the possibilities. Teacher asks children of all year groups.' Then, when children want her to read to the end of the story she refuses and moves to the word-level work. Thus she ensures children have understood the work relating to the teaching objectives and have time to assimilate this. But she does not let their enjoyment of the story persuade her to be side-tracked from the purposes of the lesson.

Mrs Harman is nowhere in our observations described as pacey. The observer wrote in her field notes,

There is no sense of urgency in this teacher's lessons, however, I do feel she's effective in pushing the children's thinking forward; because she recognises their thinking and the importance of it by listening well, by responding with thought and consideration by giving them time to think, by enlisting their help, by valuing their thoughts and remembering what they've said. Her interactions with children are respectful and supportive. Through these each child seems to experience a quality relationship.

(Field notes, April 1999)

Yet the sense of purpose in her lessons is evident. In the observation reported below she is looking at story settings and characters.

Teacher asks, 'How do you know the witch isn't nasty? Which words tell you?' The children begin to make up answers but teacher pulls them back to the text – they find 'nice', 'cuddly', 'friendly', 'comfy' and talk about each one. Teacher elaborates. Children want to read on in the story but teacher firm!

(Field notes, December 1998)

In contrast, Mrs King who was also extremely talented at engaging children and ensuring their involvement in the literacy hour often let herself follow the children's lead away from the objective of the session. For example, when reading the story of *The Ugly Duckling* with the intention of drawing attention to components of a story (beginning, middle, end), the teacher clearly had the children's interests in mind.

11.04: Teacher reads in quiet voice – asks how children would feel re: situations in story. Children comment on pictures, say how they would feel. Teacher prompts for prediction. Teacher reads with expression, asks, 'Do you think . . .?', 'I wonder . . .'

Finishing story. Children quiet and absorbed. Teacher asks questions about whether duckling is happier with swans. Children spontaneously say what's on their minds. Teacher answers or comments on each contribution.

(Observation, January 1999)

It would be wrong to criticise the above as interaction about a text as the children were engaged and the teachers' questions helped them link the text to their own experience and she valued their responses. In many ways the nature of this interaction is more of the kind valued by writers such as Wells (1987) and Wood (1986). Children are able to explore their own meanings and the role of the teacher is far less directive. There should always be a place for this kind of interaction around literacy. However, it is questionable whether it can be done well in a whole class setting and it runs counter to the focused and objectives-led philosophy of the literacy hour. It was a great disappointment to us in the research team that Mrs King's class did not make very much progress in writing and their reading test scores dropped considerably. One of the key differences between Mrs King's teaching and Mrs Harman's was the way Mrs King followed the lead of the children in exploration of texts. In the current climate the long-term benefits that may well accrue from this open-ended approach are not likely to be valued as much as short-term test results. Unfortunately, Mrs King moved on to another job after the first year of the project so we were not able to follow her class into a second year.

High expectations

One of the concerns of many teachers at the introduction of the NLS was the high expectations required by the Framework of Objectives. The amount to be covered and the speed with which this had to be done surprised many teachers. The NLS document describes the most successful teaching as being, ambitious with optimism about high expectations of success (DfEE, 1998). There was quite some difference of opinion between teachers in our study as to how realistic the NLS expectations were. They had concerns about both expectations of independence and expectations of attainment.

One of the features of the literacy hour that Mrs Harman said she felt had changed her teaching in the first year of implementation was the depth and variety of the work she covered. She described the way she had covered a much wider range of types of text than in previous years and gone into aspects of these texts in a way she would not have before.

She also explained how pleased she was with the way children had learned to be independent in their working. Mrs Harman worked hard from the beginning of the year to establish routines to enable her children to work independently. She had made signs reminding children of the five things to do before asking for help from the teacher. Keith, the year 2 target child, showed our observer the sign. He explained if he needs to find out how to spell a word he 'breaks it down' and if that does not work the sign tells him to:

1   Use dictionaries
2   Ask a friend
3   Ask another adult
4   Get on with another piece of work
5   Try again yourself.

The observer comments that the teacher seemed to be sensitive to children's needs and abilities in differentiating tasks. On the day that this comment was made the teacher was doing guided writing with a group of year 2 children. Meanwhile, one group was doing an alphabet puzzle with the support of a classroom assistant who was working with a child with special educational needs; a year 1 group was working independently sorting rhyming words; and another group worked independently reading and answering questions. On occasion she had to remind children to work quietly but this was sufficient. It seemed that familiarity with the pattern and expectations of the literacy hour made it easier for children to work within the well-established routine. At the end of year interview Mrs Harman explained how she had deliberately worked to help children to be independent.

> I think also you have got to plan the work so that they can do it independently . . . so you have got to pitch it at the right level with the right amount of challenge that's not too much difficulty or, you know, working together in pairs and helping each other so it's the way you plan the work and how you tell them they've got to behave – making them aware that they hadn't got to disturb you.'
>
> (Interview, July 1999)

She likened this to her previous practice when she was reading individually with a child and her class knew she did not want to be interrupted.

Metacognitive modelling

Modelling how readers and writers go about reading and writing is an important teaching strategy. But it is also useful to give children an insight into how readers and writers think as they read and as they compose. For example, research has shown that, whereas good readers monitor their comprehension of a text, poor or less experienced readers do not seem to recognise when the text does not make sense (e.g. Garner, 1980). By 'wondering aloud' teachers can show inexperienced readers how 'experts' question their understanding as they read. Similarly, teachers can demonstrate how writers think ahead as they write and reread what they have written. Without these common practices being made explicit they may well remain invisible to many children.

Given the opportunities for this in shared reading and writing, we were surprised how rarely we observed teachers to model their thought processes as they read or wrote with children. Mrs Harman regularly shared her thinking with children and her personal response to literacy activities. The children followed suit, relaxed and easily expressing their views on what might happen or what something could mean. On one occasion a child pointed out a sentence that started with 'and' and commented that Mrs Harman had told them not to do this. Mrs Harman took the opportunity to wonder aloud what the author was trying to do by starting a sentence with 'and'.

Metalanguage

Metalanguage, that is the language to talk about language, is a feature of the NLS Framework of Objectives. Many teachers have expressed concern about the level of language knowledge required to teach the Framework. For many teachers much of the language was new (e.g. ellipsis, morpheme) or only partially understood (e.g. adjective as a 'describing word', verb as a 'doing word'). The teachers in the project used the more familiar forms of metalanguage regularly, for example, 'full stop', and 'comma'.

Mrs Harman recognised that one of the ways in which her teaching had changed during the year was in the use of big books with the whole class. This provides the opportunity for teachers to model how we read and also to demonstrate aspects of text alongside correct terminology. For example, following the reading of *Where's My Baby*, Mrs Harman asked children to identify the first word in the questions, 'how', 'where', 'what', when', and wrote them on the board.

The example of the literacy hour given below illustrates the various forms of metalanguage that arose from one literacy hour and how it can form a natural part of classroom discussion.

10.14: Teacher and children read the text aloud as teacher points. Read with expression. Occasionally they stop to talk about what's happening in pictures. Children say what they think. Teacher makes personal responses. Teacher and children enjoy the narrative represented in pictures. Child brings up syntax point and everyone discusses, find examples in text. Compares it to poetry.

10.21: Teacher brings up point from worksheet, children had question re commas to make sense. They discuss, children give opinions, trying to make sense of text and author's motives.

10.28: Teachers writes 'fr' on white board asks children to say sounds relates to 'friends' from story. Asks children for other 'fr' words. Child suggests 'frog' – teacher says there are 4 phonemes. Draws word grid and children say letters to go in. Child suggests 'fruit', teacher helps them sound it out. Child knows 'ui'. 'Fred' Teacher keeps referring to number of phonemes. Children excited desperate to contribute.

10.35: Teacher allocates tasks and explains what they must do . . .

10.45: Teacher sits with small group, supports them in their task of changing text to 1st person. Teacher rereads passages and talks about meaning and relates to children's own life. Teacher listens to children contributions, reflects on them, comments and validates.

10.52: Child reads her list of 'fr' words. Teacher asks her where she found them. Teacher asks child to read her story about being pushed out i.e. modelled on shared story. Teacher comments on specific aspects and appreciates their individual efforts. One child is asked to read her first person version of the story.

(Observation, April 1999)

Here, the use of metalanguage provides a shared vocabulary with which teachers and children can discuss texts and enables the teacher to focus on particular aspects that she wishes to highlight. Unlike many of us who have been made afraid of the technical vocabulary of grammar, these children were enthusiastic. For children who have no difficulty in learning words such as 'tyranosaurus' and 'diplodocus', these words need cause no fears.

Unfortunately, not all use of metalanguage worked so well. It is possible that the early introduction of some more difficult concepts could lead to misunderstandings when explanations are simplified. There is an occasion when the class is reading a poem together and the teacher asks what the poet has put at the end of each line. Mrs Harman is using this to draw attention to commas separating items in a list, but some children say that commas tell you to 'swallow your breath'. Whether this explanation had come from Mrs Harman earlier or elsewhere, clearly an attempt has been made to explain the function of commas in simple, but erroneous, terms.

Ownership

For many teachers there was an initial concern about the prescriptive nature of the hour and there was a concern about how much freedom was allowed. For some teachers the timing of the hour seemed to take precedence over decisions about children's learning. These 'clock watchers' seemed inhibited by the structure whereas others moved quickly to more flexibility within the hour. Mrs Harman was concerned about aspects of the hour that she did not follow rigorously:

> I do tend to run over a bit. . . . I don't mean I run over um an hour and a half but I tend to run over rather than finish on the hour, almost invariably. . . . I think its um the group work maybe what I plan – they take longer over than they should or whether I have not planned it correctly but it's often bitty and you tend to think there are some children that haven't finished so you've got this unfinished work and you think well I'll just give them a few minutes longer to try and complete it otherwise you've got a lot of unfinished work.

> I mean I suppose when you think about it, it's not particularly the literacy hour as such. It happens in the school work [in general], isn't it? You get some children that finish work and other children that are slower and it's how to make the slower ones speed up.

(Interview, July 1999)

It will be remembered from details given above that Mrs Harman was the teacher who scored highest (i.e. most child-centred) of all the teachers in our project. It is evident that she struggled with the dilemmas that most teachers face of how to cover the curriculum and move children's learning forward at the same time as catering for the needs of the individual.

Summary

Mrs Harman, despite being a teacher whose philosophy was mainly child-centred and who had initial misgivings about the literacy hour, was successful in her teaching both in terms of observable progress and in the engagement of the children in her class. To summarise the features of her teaching that may have contributed to this, the following points seem significant:

- She was enthusiastic about the work she did with children and they responded to this with enthusiasm.
- She enjoyed the English work and her enthusiasm for the texts she used seemed to rub off on to children.
- She was very sensitive to the children's developing abilities, spending time in observing children's reactions and listening carefully to what they said.
- She used questioning and 'wondering aloud' effectively in whole class sessions to reinforce teaching points and to show how readers and writers think.
- There was a sense of purpose in her lessons. This did not appear to be over-controlling but she kept mainly to the teaching focus.
- She drew on children's previous experience in and out of school to reinforce teaching points and ensure understanding.
- She learned to be more structured and focused in her teaching without letting this overcome her concern for the individual.

Advice for Key Stage 1 teachers

Mrs Harman is a good example of a teacher who felt that her traditional, child-centred approach to teaching young children was seriously threatened by the introduction of the literacy hour. Yet she did not let this stand in the way of her relationship with her class or stop her developing as a teacher. The points that can be learned from studying Mrs Harman's experience over the two years seem to indicate the following:

- Direct teaching does not have to mean ignoring the needs of the learner. The framework can provide a useful structure to work within and it does not have to result in a transmission model of teaching.

- Good quality texts are important to motivate both teacher and children.
- Young children can learn to be independent given the appropriate support and training.
- Literacy hours should not be rushed but a sense of purpose is important.
- Watching how the teacher reads and writes, and hearing how she thinks while doing this, can help children understand the literacy process. This is as effective, if not more so, than direct instruction of skills.
- Teaching skills in the context of texts (either one to be read or one that teacher or child has written) helps give children the knowledge but also the understanding about how and when to apply the skill.
- High quality interaction can take a variety of forms depending on the purpose of the interaction. Some forms may be more appropriate in small groups or one-to-one where the outcomes are open-ended than the more focused, whole class part of the literacy hour.

7 The literacy hour at Key Stage 2

Introduction

Rather than describe a Key Stage 2 teacher whose teaching had changed following the introduction of the National Literacy Strategy, I have chosen to examine the teaching of one of the most experienced teachers in our project. Although she made some changes to her teaching over the year, it would be more true to say that her way of working had been changing for some time before the NLS. In this case it is interesting to explore how a school that was doing well in literacy teaching before the introduction of the NLS coped with the implementation of the strategy and what an experienced teacher had to say about the changes. The teacher, Mrs York, seemed to exemplify an experienced and effective teacher who worked successfully with the NLS. It is hoped that the analysis of her practice can provide a useful picture of the literacy strategy in action at Key Stage 2.

Yew Tree Primary School

Yew Tree Primary School is a small primary school in a village situated about six miles from the nearest large town. The school has been in the village for over 150 years and, until recently, served a largely farming community. Over the last few years there has been some new housing built which mostly now serves a commuter population. There were about 100 children on roll in four classes. Children, who were all white and from homes where English is the first language, came from a range of home backgrounds representing a fairly normal spread of attainment on entry to school. There are four classes in the school: reception, year 1; year 2 with the oldest year 1 children (this class was also part of the project); years 3 and 4; years 5 and 6, which was Mrs York's class.

The school had had an Ofsted inspection in the year before the introduction of the NLS. The report reflected the good progress the school had made since the appointment of the new head teacher, Mrs York, three years previously. It is described as a 'caring school, which provides a sound standard of education'. Other extracts from the report give a picture of a school that was providing a good standard of literacy work before the introduction of the NLS:

> Pupils talk confidently, take part in discussions and generally demonstrate a varied vocabulary.

> At the end of KS2, pupils read and respond keenly to a variety of texts demonstrating sound reading skills. The well organised paired and group-reading routines contribute positively to progress in reading and to pupils' interest in books.

> They write for an increasingly wide range of purposes including imaginative stories and poems, factual accounts, diary writing and interview recording. . . . The practice of re-drafting is well established.
>
> (School Ofsted Report 1997)

Mrs York

Mrs York is an experienced teacher who was also the head teacher of the school. As such she taught on 3 of the 5 days in the week. She was actively involved in external projects for the local authority as well as running the school. She had also been involved in development work in literacy in another authority before taking up her post at Yew Tree Primary. Her first experience in a small school was as Key Stage 1 teacher for two terms after moving to the country from London. She then took up a position as head teacher of a two-teacher school for four years before becoming head of Yew Tree Primary.

Her score on the Teachers' Beliefs about Literacy Questionnaire (TBALQ) was 69, which indicates a slightly less structured stance than the average score, which was 60. The score she attributed to herself was 4, which is the middle point on the 1 to 7 scale. However, the way she completed the questionnaire is in itself interesting. For most of the questions on the questionnaire she provided a brief comment, indicating that she recognised the problematic nature of the questions. In fact, for eleven of the twenty-four questions she circled 'uncertain'. This did not appear to indicate an uncertainty about her teaching, rather a certainty about the complexity of the process and the importance of different approaches for different children. For example after many of the questions to which she had responded 'disagree', she wrote 'but it is true for some children'.

Before the introduction of the NLS, she followed the school's own scheme of work but they had planned the range of texts they used from the National Literacy Project. She also had an author focus and each term children would give a book presentation in which they would talk about a book they had read. They used reading partners where the oldest children were paired with a younger child with whom they would read and share books. They had recently established group reading based on group discussion and exploration of texts. She would also hold a reading conference with a child about once a term. Non-fiction reading was mostly developed through work in other curriculum areas.

Mrs York was keen to link reading and writing. Mainly she reported they would look at the features of style in reading before going on to writing in that style. She also described their use of draft books and how children would be encouraged to talk to one another about their work. She described a typical writing lesson before the implementation of the NLS:

> I tend to introduce – we'd look at some piece of text first because it would have a focus, it might be, say, if we were writing a story, it might be something about a character that I wanted to focus on and I might look at extracts to do with the character and talk about them and I would try to draw out from the children what were the features of that piece of writing that, maybe, gave you a clear idea of what the character was like, what they looked like, how they spoke, what their personality was like. Then talk about how they were going to plan out their work. I mean sometimes I will give them a plan but other times they devise their own plans or we devise them together, and they would tend to maybe write a bit of it on their own, and then we'd come back and look at it and say, 'What did you like about this . . .?' And I would be very involved in, I suppose, supporting those who would find it hard.
>
> (Interview, July 1998)

The school had decided to focus their work for the year 1998–9 on writing as they felt this needed more work than reading. They had planned to introduce the literacy hour over the first half of the autumn term, planning from the Framework of Objectives from the beginning. They planned to start with whole class work, which would be mainly writing based and to introduce word work and the plenary as soon as possible after that. From the beginning, Mrs York recognised the importance of the plenary saying, 'I think it could drop off the end so I want to put that in straight away.' The guided and individual work was planned to be underway by the end of October. She did not anticipate their pupils having too many problems with working individually as they had been used to this during group reading in the previous year. Nevertheless, she was planning to introduce routines and strategies to help children to work independently.

Generally, Mrs York was enthusiastic about the NLS, saying she was quite excited about it as she liked new things and challenges. She also had concerns. She was worried that they would have to give up certain things that had been done in the past, such as book making. She was also concerned that it might not be suited to the most and least able children. She said, 'There's not going to be time for children to read on their own; become absorbed in books and develop and understand books. I hope we don't lose reading to children, I think that's something else that's being squeezed' (interview, July 1998).

Attainment and progress

The 1997 Ofsted report on the school described attainment in English as in line with the national average. Taking national test results over four years, attainment can be seen to have risen very slightly for the mid and top band of children (see Table 7.1).

Reading

The results from the tests that we administered at the start of the project indicated that the class had made some more progress than might be expected. At the outset of the year they scored in the range 75 to 123 with 58 per cent of the class scoring more than 100 and an average score for the class of 103. In June the following year the average score was 107, with 65 per cent of the class scoring more than 100 and a range of 77 to 135.

Writing

The two target children also made good progress in writing over the year. Both children showed imagination in their writing and developed in their use of a more literary style as can be seen in the year 6 child, Lana's writing, in Figures 7.1 and 7.2. They both increased in the number of common words spelled correctly. Lana's number of spelling errors increased during the year as her use of vocabulary became more varied but in assessment pieces she showed she could spell many words accurately. Tish, the year 5 pupil, spelled common words correctly but still transposed some letters, e.g. *hoilday*. She also had a particular problem with homophones – including the delightful 'know wear in site'! Both girls' use of connectives improved in range and type. They used full stops and capital letters consistently. Lana learned to use commas and paragraphing.

Engagement

Both target children were observed to be actively engaged in the observed literacy hours. This is despite the fact that one of the girls had some behaviour problems. Both were either attentive or contributing at each

Table 7.1 Key Stage 2 English test scores for Yew Tree Primary School (percentage at each level)

KS2	1997	1998	1999	2000
<Level 3	7	–	7	8
Level 3	20	17	27	16
Level 4	59	65	33	38
Level 5	13	6	27	38

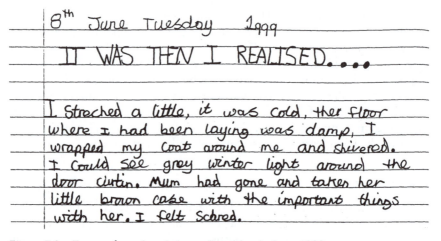

8ᵗʰ September tuesday 1998

THE CREEPY HOUSE

Tom Jones lived in dark falls. It was very dark the light's didn't work. They went back outside to collect the rest of the stuff a Girl called casey looked up at the window and saw someone up stairs they had a dog the dog saw the person upstairs and ran up the stairs. Tom said Shut up Jess "That the dog's name 'Jess'.' Tom said to casey go and get Jess from up stairs. Cosey walked slowley up th stairs "He Jess Jess come on cried" she went into one of the rooms by Jess wasent there.

Figure 7.1 Extract from Lana's (year 6) writing in September 1998.

8ᵗʰ June Tuesday 1999

IT WAS THEN I REALISED....

I streched a little, it was cold, ther floor where I had been laying was damp, I wrapped my coat around me and shivered. I could see grey winter light around the door curtin. Mum had gone and taken her little brown case with the important things with her. I felt Scared.

Figure 7.2 Extract from Lana's (year 6) writing in June 1999.

point. In fact, all children in the class always seemed to be keen to contribute and enthusiastic about what they were asked to do. One caveat to this is that Mrs York, at the end of the second year of the NLS, expressed concern about some children's attitude to reading. She was worried about the lack of opportunity for children to spend time with texts and found that many children, especially boys, seemed less likely to finish books they had taken home to read than they were before the NLS.

Teaching reading and writing in the literacy hour

Shared reading

Yew Tree Primary School already had a well-established approach to the teaching of reading as was discussed above. As our visits fell at the beginning of the week, we more usually observed shared reading than shared writing which would be more likely to take place in the second half of the week. However, a feature of Mrs York's practice was the close links between reading and writing that were evident in every literacy hour we observed. Seven of the nine literacy hours (eight in 1998–9 and one in 1999–2000) involved some shared reading of a range of different types of text according to the focus for the block of work. The type of texts read over the nine visits can be studied below:

- A newspaper article about toothpaste
- A fable
- An extract from a novel
- A narrative poem
- Letters
- Another poem
- Tourist pamphlets.

In the first literacy hour we observed, the text was an enlarged photo-copy that was hung on a flip chart. After this it was more usual for children to be given a photocopy of the text between two. When the tourist pamphlets were used Mrs York gave a pamphlet to each child. Each child having their own (or shared) copy of the text meant that they had some-thing to hold, there was no danger of poor eyesight causing difficulties, or of other children getting in the way. However, there was no chance for Mrs York to point to the piece of text that was being discussed or to ensure that all children were focused on the same section. This meant that less able readers, although they would have benefited from hearing a challenging text read aloud, may not have been able to follow the words as they were read.

A key feature of all Mrs York's interactions with children around texts was her clear focus on meaning. Although each lesson had objectives based on those in the Framework of Objectives, she was always keen to ensure that children understood what they were reading and that they could relate this to their own experience. A shared reading session in the literacy hour observed in May is typical. The session was based around looking at the different viewpoints of characters using *The Jolly Postman* by Janet and Alan Ahlberg. The objective for this part of the lesson was given as 'to revise different styles/formats of letters'. The lesson related to the text level objectives for year 5 about different points of view (Y5T3T2 and 7) and the objectives relating to impersonal, formal language in year 6 (Y6T3S3 and T16).

9.19: Teacher lays out what they are doing this week i.e. revising how different people in a situation have different viewpoints. Teacher focuses on versions of the *Three Little Pigs* and incidents in the playground i.e. [teacher] listening to both parties [points of view]. Teacher shows *Jolly Postman* books, takes out letters etc. to remind children. She gives photocopies of three letters from *The Jolly Postman* and the children are to identify how they are different and similar. Children to talk to their partners. They are given a couple of minutes. She asks children to read aloud letter 1, identified as 'formal'.

9.26: Teacher asks another child to read letter 2 then letter 3. When children get stuck with words Teacher asks the whole class 'Who can work that out?' She asks what differences between 1 and 2, informal versus formal. Children identify lots of mistakes and different endings. Teacher writes different ways to end a letter on white board and children identify which are formal and which informal. She asks children to think of examples of letters you might write where you might not know the name of the people/person you are writing to, [and so need to use] 'Yours faithfully'. Children generate ideas.

9.33: Teacher prompts for more differences among the three letters. She wants children to look closely at details in letters i.e. signature followed by name typed out, use of P. S., use of computer versus hand-written. She draws attention to headed paper. She prompts for writing address and date and position on page. She gives children 2 minutes to correct *Goldilocks* letter (2) and underline hard words and phrases in other two letters. She reminds them they have only a short time.

(Observation, May 1999)

Although in this session, she did not read any of the letters aloud while the class followed the text, in other ways this shared text level part of the literacy hour was typical of all such sessions we observed in Mrs York's class. There are the following features which seem to combine the principles of the model of literacy teaching as proposed by the NLS and include elements of what could also be considered as good primary practice:

- Reading and writing are linked
- Work is based on high quality text
- The teacher retains a focus on the objectives
- The pace is good with an insistence on moving on
- The session is interactive with pupils' contributions encouraged and extended
- The teacher has high expectations of the children's contributions.

In addition:

- The period is broken up by short, focused tasks in which every child is actively involved

- The meaning of the text is paramount and related to children's own experience
- Children are encouraged to be active problem solvers.

Guided reading

We also observed guided reading on five occasions. Whereas their earlier group reading project had mainly involved discussion about texts, guided reading after the introduction of the NLS also included some reading aloud by individual children. The same pattern carried on all year. A typical session took place in January when a small group of four of the lowest achieving children read from *Sharron and Darren* by Nigel Gray and Cathy Wilcox.

> 9.50: Teacher reminds children where they are in the story – asks children what characters are feeling and comprehension questions. Children read out loud one at a time. Teacher compliments reading. Teacher asks questions and draws attention to features in the pictures. She follows text with finger and watches children reading – quick pace. She also checks rest of class regularly and tells children to get on.

> 9.57: Discussing what a 'demonstration' is – vocabulary in story. Children continue to read aloud individually, stops to clarify meaning of phrases. Asks children to help reader if stuck. Children involved and absorbed in their reading and story. Teacher asks which bit is their favourite and why. Children refer a lot to the drawings.
>
> (Observation, January 1999)

Shared writing

Although of the eight visits in the first year on only two occasions did we observe shared writing, writing was a regular feature of shared text work. Mrs York would use the whiteboard to write key points from reading or discussion. These points would be referred to regularly. Whilst this writing was not part of the planned teaching for the day, it demonstrated effectively an important use for writing and enabled children to see written language being produced.

We also observed two shared writing sessions. For example, in one lesson her objectives were to 'review features of script writing using panto script from yesterday. Start writing script – incorporating lay out, stage directions, etc. Start to mark for actors what's needed.' This relates to the Framework of Objectives for year 5 (T1T5, 18, 19 and 20) and year 6 (T1T9).

> 9.24: Teacher writing list of what information a playscript gives you i.e. brackets – stage directions; name of speaker on left; setting – at the beginning of the scene; characters – way they move, costumes, way

they talk. Teacher taking suggestions from children, asks for clarification of ideas, challenges ideas. Good pace – teacher refers to previous work. Teacher asks for acting example i.e. come onto the stage in a 'nervous' way. Child volunteers.

9.31: Teacher writing on flip chart Scene 1 of *Three Little Pigs* demonstrating features of playscript i.e. setting – a small cramped cottage (enter . . .)

Mother Pig: . . .

Children give ideas. Teacher questions, challenges, considers, clarifies, acts as scribe.

(Observation, December 1998)

Guided writing

We observed guided writing twice over the year and again in the follow-up visit at the end of the second year. Each time, the whole class had been set a writing task following on from the text-level work and Mrs York worked closely with one group to support or extend their writing. The sessions were used to reinforce objectives covered in the earlier session. For example, during guided writing with the highest achieving group when children were writing their own versions of letters, Mrs York talked to them about their ideas but also encouraged them to make their own decisions about what to write. She also questioned them about their use of formal or informal language. She was quick to notice what children were doing and insistent on them focusing on the task but with interaction and support. This was typical of her use of guided writing as we observed it:

- The group was selected according to ability in relation to the writing task (not a fixed grouping).
- The work was similar to that of the rest of the class but guided time was used to extend, support or reinforce the work of the shared session.
- Teaching was related to meaning as well as to form.
- Children were encouraged to make their own decisions about their writing.
- She set a brisk pace, insisting children stay on task but providing support.

Sentence- and word-level work

In her interview before the introduction of the literacy hour, Mrs York placed more emphasis on the range of texts children read and the process and content of writing than on sentence and word level. When prompted she admitted that they did not do a lot of work on grammar unless it arose from a child's writing and only occasional sessions on punctuation. For spelling they used 'look, cover, write, check' and taught children to use a dictionary and check their own work for spelling and punctuation.

From the beginning this section of the literacy hour presented problems for Mrs York. In informal discussion she mentioned that she found that choosing sentence-level objectives that related to the shared text limited the choice of appropriate, high-quality text. She also said she found it hard to fit the word or sentence level into the literacy hour and to maintain the coherence of the session. Indeed, this was apparent in some of the observed literacy hours where the shift from text to sentence or word was very abrupt. As though aware of this, whenever possible she would select as a starting point a word from the text or include it in a sentence based on the previous text. It also seemed significant that this section of the literacy hour was sometimes omitted and usually much shorter than the text-level part. Even so, in the interview at the end of the first year, she commented that she felt she had done more grammar work during the year than previously. Unfortunately, Mrs York had moved on from Yew Tree Primary School before the introduction of the Grammar for Writing materials so it is not possible to report whether she found this approach more useful.

Independent work

From before the introduction of the literacy hour, Yew Tree Primary School had done quite a lot of group work so Mrs York was not over-concerned about how her class would manage working independently. However, the school worked from the start of the year on strategies for making sure children had all the things they needed at the start of the independent time to avoid distraction from unnecessary movement. She commented 'So I think from September that come hell or high water you stay in your place. We've come up with things that we will need to have available to each of the children' (interview, July 1998).

On each visit the independent work observed was similar. It always involved a piece of writing. This might be the start of a longer piece of writing as, for example, when children began to draft work on their own fable following the shared reading of a fable on Monday and, on the Tuesday, shared reading focusing on the characteristics of a fable. More usually, short pieces of writing based on the shared reading or writing were set; for example, following the shared reading of three poems, children were to write their own short poem based on a similar format to one of the given poems. On only one occasion was the independent work something different or based on the word-level work. On this day, following work on note taking and opposites, children had to finish off a text marking activity and then extend a list of opposites that they had started in the whole class session. At no time was the class observed working from work books or using photocopiable sheets.

Plenary

Mrs York emphasised from the outset that she thought the plenary was important but raised the concern that it would be easy to let it 'drop off the end'. In all the observed sessions, Mrs York held a plenary and reiterated the importance of it in the end of year interview saying 'I think the plenary's good. I think it has been really interesting because . . . That's the bit the kids listen most carefully to because it is often the children talking to each other (um) and it has been quite fascinating' (interview, July 1999).

The plenary in Mrs York's class tended to be the time children got to share the writing they had done in the independent part of the hour. The lesson plans for the literacy hours that we observed always identified which aspect of the children's work would be emphasised. This emphasis was more apparent on some days than others. However, Mrs York always used the time to praise children who had worked well in the independent time and to point out (or let the children themselves point out) what was good or interesting in their work. This usually referred back to the objectives for the literacy hour but could also reflect other relevant but unplanned aspects. An example can be found after the literacy hour in which children explored the content and performance of narrative poems and had been asked to write their own brief poems. In the plenary on this occasion some children read out unfinished poems and Mrs York encouraged discussion about what would happen next in the narrative. Another time following the writing of letters, Mrs York had planned to focus on specific stylistic features but instead asked the class who had written something they were really pleased with and she made mainly general comments. The observer noted 'Most [children] appear really pleased with themselves' (field notes, May 1999).

Relationship with the class

Like most of the teachers in this project, Mrs York had an excellent relationship with her class. Although, as a busy head teacher involved in activities beyond the school as well as within it she spent many days outside the classroom, the class worked enthusiastically for her. She, herself, said she found it difficult to maintain consistency of expectation with her frequent absences. However, our observations point to children being well behaved and improving as the year progressed in their ability to work independently and purposefully while the teacher worked with a group.

Questioning

A key feature of the observations of Mrs York's teaching is the repeated comments by the observer on the quality of her interaction with pupils. This was evidenced by general observations that the children all seemed to be involved and by observation of the target children who were also normally observed to be actively involved in the lesson. When commenting on the shared reading and discussion of fables, the observer wrote after the lesson,

> Teacher asked the children what they think the meaning is, encouraging to express their ideas and opinions. She supports them in their attempts and if need be she extends the ideas. Really had feeling that children on the whole feel free to practise expressing thoughts and ideas. Therefore almost everyone does, but with hands up. . . . Teacher seems to have high expectations of the children and values their contributions.
>
> (Field notes, January 1999)

Mrs York was observed to use questions in different ways to suit her purposes, mixing open and closed questions, as appropriate. When working with a high achieving group in the guided reading of a poem, the observer noted this differential use of questioning.

> Teacher asks for children's first impressions and if they understand it. Teacher asks specific questions about the poem and encourages all the group to participate. Teacher asks lots of open and exploratory questions and challenges children to look more closely at the rhythm in different verses.
>
> (Field notes, February 1999)

Criticism has been levelled against classroom interaction, particularly in whole class situations, in that rather than encouraging thinking it closes down discussion and presents the teacher as main arbiter (Wells, 1987). Moyles *et al.* (2000) comment on the inconsistency implied in 'direct interactive teaching, with whole classes or groups' (Beard, 1999: 20). They argue that the effect of increasing the number of contacts is potentially counter-productive in the development of higher order exchanges. Indeed Mroz *et al.* (2000) in an analysis of the discourse styles of ten teachers in the literacy hour found pupils were given little opportunity to question or explore ideas. Wells (1999) identifies reasons for the apparent contradiction between those who praise 'quality interaction' as something that is attainable in whole class, direct teaching situations and those who see it as impossible. He argues that the viewpoints arise from two very different views of the purposes of education. Those who endorse the use of direct interactive teaching with whole classes are those who are concerned with the responsibility of ensuring that students 'appropriate the artefacts and practices that embody the solutions to problems encountered in the past' (p. 168). Whereas he argues that those who criticise this form of question–answer interaction arise from those who see education as a means of 'cultural renewal and for the formation and empowerment of its individual members to deal effectively with future problems' (ibid.). Wells goes on to argue that this form of triadic dialogue is not in itself wrong but depends upon the purposes for which it is used.

It seems to me that Mrs York seemed to go some way towards achieving direct interactive teaching with the whole class without giving the impression of being the only judge of what is valued. The quality of this interaction seems to stem from two features. First, the respect that Mrs York showed for children's contributions in the way she allowed them time to answer and avoided closing down each topic after one or two 'correct' responses. Second, she used open questions that allowed for a range of answers rather than the one right one but also used language to direct the interaction through questioning, clarifying ideas, challenging ideas and generally facilitating discussion.

High expectations

Many features of the teaching in this classroom point to high expectations of children's performance and behaviour. These features include the following:

- The expectation that children can make decisions for themselves.
- The expectation that work will be completed and to a high standard.
- Children's contributions are valued and complimented, e.g. 'Well I know if C. says it's "lordly" then I know I'm on the right track'.
- Contributions are not always accepted, for example, if they do not make sense.
- Use of appropriate metalanguage.
- The expectation that all children will be able to interpret texts beyond the literal meaning, including author's opinion and hidden agenda.
- The use of challenging and varied texts and vocabulary.

Mrs York was a teacher who we identified at the start of the year as being knowledgeable about literacy. She was the literacy co-ordinator for her school and had been involved in language projects beyond her own school over several years. This confidence and familiarity with metalanguage was a feature of her teaching and something that passed on to her class. Not only were terms such as: verb, past tense, pronoun, prefix, preposition and so on used correctly and routinely in this classroom but other terms were discussed from the beginning of the year. Ideas such as stereotypes, style, formal and informal language. The texts she used also contained challenging ideas and interesting vocabulary, for example the fable discussed in the second literacy hour contained items such as, 'as ill luck would have it', 'revenge is a two-edged sword', 'set his wits to work' and so on.

Change to teaching of literacy

When asked at the end of the second year of the literacy strategy how she felt her teaching had changed, Mrs York replied that she felt she had become more 'focused, structured and specific' than she had been before. She also said that she was unable to identify where changes in her teaching had originated. She felt that some changes had been evolving over the couple of years leading up to the introduction of the NLS. She also argued that the focus on literacy that the school had identified had involved them in a range of initiatives, all of which had contributed to a gradual and on-going development of teaching style.

Focused teaching

Mrs York attributed her increased concern to make objectives clear to children to her training as an Ofsted inspector rather than the NLS. However, a subtle change can be observed in the planning over the first year of the NLS. In the first term, her written plans were divided into the sections of the hour with learning objectives and what children will do mixed in together. By the end of the first year, she had adopted the practice of listing the objective for each section of the hour at the beginning of the plan and then outlining what would happen in each section of the lesson. In addition, the range of the objectives covered in one session was reduced. We found it interesting to note those teachers who summarised the objectives on their lesson plan as opposed to those who just noted the reference numbers from the Framework of Objectives. We surmised from this that it was more likely that teachers would focus on the objective if it was fresh in their mind in their plan for the day than if they had merely copied a number from another planning sheet.

Mrs York's lesson plan for the first half of the first literacy hour observed in November shows both the mixing of objectives and activity and the range of objectives covered.

> <u>Intro</u> – Review yesterday's work.
>
> <u>Text</u> – newspaper report – longer – shared copies. Emphasis – how report put together. Use of paragraphs. Untangling meaning. Headlines – use of.
>
> <u>Word/sentence</u> – tenses of verbs – particularly past. Changing sentence from present to past. What has to change? Different forms of past – ed addition, use of auxiliary. Unusual forms.
>
> (Lesson plan, 3 November 1998)

The plan for the last lesson we observed in the first year shows the change in planning.

Objectives – work on poetry

Text – to read, rehearse and modify performance of poetry.

Sentence – extend work on prepositions.

Text – Child from the Future. Read and discuss 'story' of the poem. How could it be performed – using punctuation etc.

Sentence – work on prepositions, identifying how use changes meaning.
(Lesson plan, 13 July 1999)

The text-level part of the first lesson covers the years 5 and 6, text-level objectives about the features of texts such as reports (Y5T1T21) and (Y6T1T12,13), including concern for layers of meaning and layout which are also features of year 6 text-level work. The same section of the July lesson relates to just one year 5 objective, although there were other poetry objectives from the third term for both year 5 and year 6 but they are not used in this lesson. The work on the poem emphasises the meaning and intention of the poet, as with all Mrs York's lessons but the focus is clearly on how this impacts on the performance of the poem.

Pace

Medwell *et al.* (1998) found that their effective teachers of literacy conducted their lessons at a brisk pace. These teachers regularly refocused children's attention and used clear time-frames for children to work within, ending lessons with a review of what they had done during the lesson. The clear time-frame for the work and the plenary are, of course, features of the literacy hour but pace was, certainly, a feature of Mrs York's teaching.

Pace was one aspect of teaching that we, as a research team, disagreed on. We debated the extent to which pace was a good thing that moved children forward or a bad thing that inhibited reflection and caused anxiety. We also debated whether, if a brisk pace were appropriate, were it so for all children from the age of 5. Certainly there were days when Mrs York as a busy head teacher seemed almost rushed in her urgency to move the lesson on. However, more usually the observer's comments reflected a sense of moving children forward in their thinking as well as keeping them on task. The following extracts from the field notes for three literacy hours are representative of comments in all Mrs York's lessons.

4.5.99   Teacher's pace was insistent with expectation, everything seemed to have a purpose.

21.6.99   Teacher brisk, businesslike, with purpose

13.7.99   Teacher keeps a good brisk pace. Short, child-involved [sic] tasks in pairs, in groups and whole class discussion. Teacher signals time limits and sets clear expectations. High degree of interaction.

It seemed that Mrs York was able to maintain a purposeful atmosphere in the classroom without this becoming overly pressurised. The frequent opportunities she afforded children for discussion in pairs or small groups ensured that they were able to have some time to explore their own ideas.

Metacognitive modelling

As discussed earlier, we had hoped to observe examples of metacognitive modelling in the literacy hour. There should be many opportunities in shared reading and writing for the teacher to show children how experienced readers and writers think while they are reading and writing. Although Mrs York did not make explicit reference to her thinking as she read or wrote in front of the class, there were times when her thinking was made clear to the children. When she was scribing children's composition of a playscript, she listened to their contributions and gave reasons why she was rejecting some. This was useful as a means of showing her reasoning but had the inherent danger of appearing that the teacher is the sole arbiter of writing in school. This voicing of the writer's thoughts is important in the context of demonstrating writing, where the teacher models the control the writer has over their own writing. This is subtly different from giving reasons why one child's idea is preferable to another.

On the whole, Mrs York used questioning as a technique to prompt children's thinking about their writing and reading. We did not note any examples where she used 'wondering loud' as a way of eliciting responses that would also have modelled to children her thoughts as a writer or reader. It is possible that a technique such as 'wondering aloud' where reflection is encouraged, might create a different classroom atmosphere than the brisk and purposeful one that was Mrs York's. However, children in her class always seemed confident in their contributions and eager to argue their point of view.

Ownership

It must already be clear to readers that Mrs York was a teacher who was already teaching to some extent in the style of the NLS. She welcomed the initiative and, whilst having some misgivings, was eager to take it on. Two years on, her style of teaching seemed very similar to what it had been before with the developments that are discussed above. However, she seemed confident to adapt the structure and content to suit what she felt were the needs of her class. She did this in a number of ways:

* In the first term of the first year they introduced extended writing on the fifth day of the week.
* Some text-level objectives were blocked and taught 'in bursts' rather than being a regular feature of the literacy hour.

- She developed the use of targets and checklists as reminders for individual children for some aspects of word-level work involving the teaching of individuals during writing sessions.
- She reordered some of the objectives to match certain text types in a way that worked better for her.

Despite this she still felt that children no longer had enough opportunity to spend time on texts or to study them at length. Although she had tried in the early part of the second year to find more time for this she had found 'other things took over.'

Summary

Overall the impression we gained of Mrs York was that of an enthusiastic and successful teacher: a teacher who was already using many of the elements stressed by the NLS as features of good teaching. The introduction of the literacy hour made only slight changes to the way she taught – some that she felt were for the good and some that she felt less positive about. Over the two years there was little change in the way she interacted with children or in the content of her teaching. She remained a teacher who concentrated emphatically on the meaning of the texts they read or wrote together. She continued to encourage children to be confident, enthusiastic and independent in their use of literacy. She continued to introduce new ideas and initiatives into her class and her school, not allowing herself or her staff to sit back and rely on the literacy strategy but always looking for new ways to bring the best out of the children. But as well as this she felt the literacy strategy and the other initiatives she had been involved with had made her more 'focused, structured and specific' in her teaching of literacy. If there are identifiable features of a good teacher to be drawn from the case of Mrs York they can be summarised as follows:

- She approached new ideas with enthusiasm, determined to make the best of them.
- She was prepared to adapt ideas to fit her teaching and her understanding of her class and of literacy.
- She had a good working knowledge of the elements of the literacy strategy and how language works.
- She emphasised meaning and purpose over and above other aspects of reading and writing.
- She recognised and planned for the essential link between reading and writing.
- She was focused in her teaching of specific elements of reading and writing.
- She kept up a good pace in her teaching both within each lesson and in what she taught.

- She taught aspects of language such as grammar, despite her misgivings.
- She approached the aspects of literacy she was teaching with an enthusiasm, which the children reflected in their response.
- She responded with enthusiasm to children's own reading and writing.
- She had high expectations of behaviour and attainment.
- She encouraged children to express their own ideas and respect each other's – and she did the same for theirs.
- She related the reading and writing being taught to children's own lives.

Advice for teachers at Key Stage 2

Mrs York was largely enthusiastic about the NLS after two years, although she did not feel it was the only influence on the way her teaching had developed over several years. Her attitude to the NLS and her style of teaching point to various features of successful teaching in the literacy hour:

- A good working knowledge of the subject and the structure of the framework enables more effective and flexible teaching.
- Drawing attention to specific features of language should be done with the purpose and meaning of the text in mind: for example, showing how the author's use of adjectives influence our opinion of a character.
- Good pace means more than being quick. It implies a sense of purpose and a desire to achieve. It makes good use of setting short activities within clear time frames that children understand clearly. But it also involves these time-constrained activities being part of a larger sense of purpose building to something over a week or longer.
- High-quality interaction in whole class settings may imply pace and higher order questioning, but there must also be a place for the child's ideas and reflection on learning. There is a fine balance between control and direction; that is between the teacher being seen as the only arbiter of what is valued in literacy and as the expert leading and supporting the learner.
- While working with good quality texts in the literacy hour is essential, it is also important to consider the whole of the child's reading experience. Children should have the opportunity to hear or to read good quality texts for pleasure. Reflection and sustained concentration are also key features of literacy behaviour.

8 The literacy hour in mixed-age classes

Introduction

The original impetus for this research project was to examine how the literacy strategy worked in mixed-age classes so it seems strange that a chapter specifically about mixed-age classes should not appear until now. As I described earlier, we found that most of the findings from the research were applicable to all classes and not only relevant to classes where there was more than one year group. Having said that, there were points that came out from the research that are particularly relevant to mixed-age groups, although we found no blueprint for working with mixed-age classes. Teachers tried many different strategies, particularly in relation to the choice of objectives. There was no agreed 'best way', rather some general principles that seemed to be useful in underpinning the choices teachers made.

Teaching and learning in mixed-age classes

Vertically grouped classes have been used from choice in primary schools for many years. Family grouping as it has been called was valued within a child-centred education system because it could draw on the very advantages of learning in the family. Young children in a mixed-age class can draw on the support of more mature and experienced learners. The older children can develop a sense of responsibility and, indeed, gain benefits in their own understanding through their interactions with the younger children. A sense of community and mutual support could be a feature of family-grouped classes. Katz *et al.* (1990) describe the mixed-age group as potentially a very rich educative environment, claiming both social and cognitive benefits. They argue that 'supportive social contexts create new levels of competence' (p. 26).

This picture seems very far removed from today's outcome-oriented, standards-driven primary schools. The kind of features valued in the paragraph above, are considered secondary to the drive to raise academic standards. For this reason, few large schools now choose to organise classes in mixed-aged groups. Where they do they are likely to teach literacy and numeracy in either ability or age group sets. And those schools that do choose mixed-age class groups will only put two year groups together, not three or four year groups as is unavoidable in some small schools.

Mixed-age classes have always been seen as having both positive and negative features. Bell and Sigsworth (1987) examined case studies of teachers in small rural primary schools. They comment that these teachers saw mixed-age classes as an advantage in that this ensured that teachers planned for a differentiated curriculum and children spent more time working independently. Flexibility is seen as an important feature of planning in mixed-age classes. Vulliamy and Webb (1995) found that teachers needed to be very flexible in their teaching. One teacher likened her teaching to spinning plates, another said 'I'm quite prepared to sort of scrap any plans for a particular age group if it's proving too difficult to get effective work from the younger ones' (p. 31). Hopkins and Ellis (1991) also emphasise the need for flexible approaches:

> In mixed-age range classes teaching approaches need to be flexible and based largely on individual and small group activities rather than on class lessons. The most effective teachers seem to be those who attempt to create a positive learning environment suited to vertical grouping by taking an individual and co-operative approach, which exploits the great variety of interactions between the different age groups in the class.
>
> (Hopkins and Ellis, 1991: 119)

These views are further reinforced by Harber (1996) who again identifies flexibility as an important factor in successful teaching and learning in small schools:

> Teachers need to ensure their teaching methods are appropriate and relevant. In mixed-age classes teaching approaches need to be flexible and based largely on individual and small group activities rather than on class lessons. Teachers therefore need to be reflective and should continually re-examine and evaluate their teaching strategies. The school should therefore have a well considered policy on mixed-age teaching.
>
> (Harber, 1996: 21)

Researchers and commentators on small schools have largely agreed that for vertical grouping to be effective, teachers have to be flexible in their approach to classroom organisation. This flexibility is difficult to achieve with a prescribed set of objectives for each year group.

The move away from an individualised approach in primary schools to more group and whole class teaching was regarded with concern by those interested in small schools. In response to the Secretary of State for Education's letter to all primary schools emphasising the desirability of whole class teaching (January 1993), Vulliamy and Webb (1995) comment, 'In the context of small schools, where all classes are mixed-age, much of this advice can be viewed as, at best, irrelevant and, at worst, counter-productive to effective learning' (p. 26). Many of the teachers studied in Galton and Patrick (1990) were cautious about whole class teaching in small schools. One headteacher reflected the views of many when he said,

> in lessons you tend to aim at the middle, which means that you are not stimulating the brighter pupils and you've lost the less able ones – so despite the fact that class teaching is a time saver in many ways, it isn't a practical solution a lot of the time.
>
> (Galton and Patrick, 1990: 36)

When we look at the attainments of children in small schools there is conflicting evidence. The PRISMS Project (Curriculum Provision in Small Primary Schools) found that children in small primary schools seemed to do as well, if not better, on standardised tests of reading, language and mathematics (Galton and Patrick, 1990). However, HMI (DES, 1978) examined the relationship between attainment on standardised tests of reading and mathematics and vertical grouping. They found significant differences in favour of single-age classes. They judged there to be clear evidence from their survey that the performance of children in vertically grouped classes can suffer. It is also suggested that many teachers find it difficult to teach classes of more than twenty-five children whose ages are spread over two or more years. DES (1982) also concluded that mixed-age classes present difficulties for very many teachers and go on to add that in the survey they noticed that both the more and less able within the class could suffer some neglect. Galton *et al.* (1980) reported similar results but found the differences between vertically grouped classes and single-age classes disappeared when teaching style was considered in the analysis. Galton and Patrick (1990) conclude 'Poor performance, therefore, may not necessarily be a result of vertical grouping as such but of the use of inappropriate forms of classroom organisation and teaching strategies with such groups' (p. 12).

Linking differences in attainment to differences in teaching approach is also indicated in The First School Survey (DES, 1982). This also concluded that where the needs of all children were not being met in mixed-age classes 'this was due sometimes to an inappropriate programme'. In impos-ing one particular organisational structure, in prescribing timed sessions of whole class and group teaching and in having a clearly defined programme of study, the introduction of the NLS appeared to be removing the flexibility of teachers to choose appropriate methods for their particular context.

Teachers' views about teaching mixed-age classes – a survey

Thoughts in 1998

Given the views expressed above it is surprising that a small survey of 100 small school teachers before the implementation of the NLS (Fisher and Lewis, 1999) found teachers to be as enthusiastic as they were about the introduction of the literacy hour. In July 1998, a sample of 104 teachers from small schools were asked to respond to a questionnaire asking what they felt most positive about and what they felt most negative about in the NLS. Overwhelmingly, teachers voiced general concerns about the literacy hour that were not peculiar to small schools and mixed-age classes. More details of this survey can be found in Chapter 10. The main concern in relation to small schools was that of the difficulty of planning and/or delivering the framework of objectives to mixed-age classes. Yet only eighteen of the 104 teachers mentioned this, less than 18 per cent. Only four remarked on the difficulty of whole class teaching with mixed-age classes and only one commented on the difficulty of selecting texts to read with a mixed-age group. Six teachers were concerned that it would be difficult to provide sufficiently challenging independent activities. They felt that this was more difficult in a mixed-age class as you would have to prepare different activities for different year groups and time pressures would make them resort to 'mundane' worksheets. The only other concern that was voiced by six of the thirty-seven Key Stage 1 teachers who responded was the difficulty of catering for the needs of the 4-year-olds in a literacy hour.

To our surprise, the teachers on the main project did not voice particular concerns about the literacy hour in relation to small schools. There was a variety of attitudes represented but not one teacher said in the initial interview that they thought the literacy hour was unsuitable for small schools. It may, of course have been that they did not wish to appear negative about work in small schools knowing the focus of our project. However, this did not stop some of them strongly voicing concerns about the NLS in general. It may also have been that the issue of meeting the needs of a wide range of age and ability was such a normal matter for these teachers that they did not see it as especially worse with the NLS. Indeed, they seemed mainly to welcome the extra support and resources provided.

Two teachers mentioned that they were concerned about the most able and less able in the class, and although this may have been made more acute because of the wide age span, neither mentioned the age of children just their ability. Mrs Ibbotsen expressed concern about catering appropriately for the 4-year-olds while teaching the literacy hour to years 1 and 2. Only Mr Piper mentioned that he found word- and sentence-level work more hierarchical and therefore thought that this would be more difficult for a wide age range.

Views in 2000

After two years of the NLS another questionnaire was given out to a similar group of teachers (sixty-one) from small schools. Again they were asked what they liked most and what they liked least about the NLS. The results of this can also be examined in more detail in Chapter 10. These teachers reflected the views of the project teachers in that they were more concerned about the teaching of literacy in general than about concerns in relation to mixed-age classes. Even fewer teachers mentioned this as a concern (see Table 8.1).

Aspects of the hour

Overwhelmingly, text level or shared reading/writing was cited as the part of the hour teachers liked.

Of those who did not like the sentence-level work, active/passive was mentioned particularly as being very difficult to teach. Equally, there was a lot of agreement about the difficulty of doing guided work. Sometimes comments related to the management of groups, other times to the difficulty of forming homogenous groups in small, mixed-age classes. Only four teachers said they did guided reading outside the hour, although an impression formed from talking to teachers was that this was more common. The plenary was also unpopular. There appeared to be a feeling for some teachers that it had no purpose. The lack of understanding of the summarising and reinforcing function of the plenary was illustrated by one teacher who said she used it to introduce the next day's work.

Framework of objectives

There were mixed feelings about the Framework of Objectives – although these were not necessarily contradictory. Some teachers mentioned it as an

Table 8.1 Teachers' views of the literacy hour in small schools in 1998 and 2000

Aspect of NLS	Percentage of teachers concerned in 1998[a]	Percentage of teachers concerned in 2000[b]
Difficulty of planning for mixed age classes	18	⎫
Difficulty of teaching the whole class	8	⎬ 10
		⎭
Challenge of finding appropriate independent work	6	5
Inappropriate for the needs of the 4 year old	16	19

Notes: [a]*n*=104.
   [b]*n*=61.

answer to both questions. Teachers who liked the Framework mentioned how helpful it was to have a structure and a focus. They appreciated having progression clearly laid out to help with planning. Teachers who did not like it referred to the 'bittiness' and said they found it too 'rigid'. Some argued that it was too inflexible. Teachers mentioned liking the variety of text types they were now using. Planning was still seen as very time-consuming. However, one teacher commented on how she found the planning of blocks of work very helpful. Teachers who liked the pace referred to the high expectations of progression and that their teaching had become sharper. Teachers who did not like it complained that there was too much to be covered too quickly.

As a teaching approach

Of these sixty-one teachers from small schools, only six mentioned that they thought the NLS was inappropriate for mixed-age classes. Two teachers mentioned they adapted the hour. One did two literacy hours in a day and another, with a four year group class, did a 'staggered' literacy hour over 1½ hours, whereby she started two year groups' whole class work and then did a second set of whole class work while the first group was working independently. There was some criticism that the NLS took away the opportunity to be spontaneous. But others mentioned how much children enjoyed it. The main criticism after two years was of a lack of time for extended writing and the fact that the 20-minute slot seemed to result in unfinished or scrappy pieces of work. Two teachers said they felt that the literacy hour inhibited independence by making children over-reliant on adults. Some Key Stage 1 teachers still felt that it was unsuitable for the youngest children.

Teaching mixed-age classes in the project schools

Progress

Children in all types of classes made progress over the year of the project. In the results of the reading tests there was found to be no statistical difference between children's progress in classes with more year groups. Having said this, four of the five classes that had four year groups were in the bottom half of a list of average progress. Equally, five of the eight classes with only two year groups were in the top half. Three of the seven classes whose children made good progress in writing contained the whole of one key stage. This seemed to confirm what teachers reported to us – that it was harder to teach all four year groups in the literacy hour. However, the number of year groups in the class did not seem to make any difference in the level of engagement of children. The three highest scores for engagement at both Key Stage 1 and at Key Stage 2 were represented by two, three, and four year group classes.

Teachers' views

The teachers in our project, like the ones from the questionnaire survey, had a whole range of thoughts about the NLS – most of these were not particularly related to teaching mixed-age classes. In order to examine the literacy hour specifically in relation to mixed-age groups, they were all asked at the end of the first year what would be the main piece of advice they would pass on to other teachers of mixed-age classes.

Figure 8.1 summarises the key points of this advice. Most points have been included. Only omitted are those from teachers who had clearly had a very difficult year and it was felt by the research team that their advice, whilst helpful to the individual teacher in the first year, would not be helpful to others who have had more experience with the literacy hour.

Choice of objectives and planning

At the start of the project we had thought the planning for multiple year groups would present the most problems for teachers. Certainly, this did

---

General
It is not possible to work out a blueprint that will work from year to year. It will change each year depending on the make up of the particular class.
High expectations are very important.

Whole class teaching
Keep objectives focused – do not try to cover every year group.
Use targeted and focused questioning.
Use a variety of texts to ensure covering all abilities and interests. Both challenging and simple with appropriate support/extension.
Children enjoy trying out things they have seen older groups do.
Plan ahead for the diferentiated questions you will use.

Independent work
It is even more important with mixed-age classes to develop independent working to ensure appropriate task demand.
Flexible grouping using pairs and co-operative work makes the most of the advantages of mixed-age classes.
It is important for reception children to have opportunity for play based activities.
With a mixed-age class you can be more relaxed about what the younger children (Key Stage 1) are doing as you know you can push them harder next year.
Independent work should be at an easier level than the shared work as it is done independently.

Guided reading/writing
Some guided work is better done outside the hour as well as during to allow for a number of small groups of children at similar levels.

Figure 8.1   Key points for mixed-age classes.

present some problems but they by no means seemed to cause the most anxiety. Two reasons seem possible here. The first may be that as experienced teachers of mixed-age classes, these teachers were used to catering for a range of needs and did not regard it as such an obstacle as those on the outside thought it might be. Another reason could be that teachers were more preoccupied with the structure of the hour and the practical concerns of organising the class in a literacy hour than with the pedagogical issue of the management of objectives. Other evidence from the interviews with teachers points to the latter as, at least playing some part in the explanation for this apparent lack of major concern about planning.

The Local Education Authority had advised small schools to teach to the objectives of the lower of two year groups. That is a teacher who had year 5 and year 6 would teach year 5 objectives in the first year and year 6 in the second year. A class that had years 3 to 6 should teach mainly year 5 objectives while 'dipping into' year 3 in the first year. The expectation here then was that in the following year the objectives relating to the higher of the two year groups would be taught. This is in contrast to some other LEAs who had advised their teachers of mixed-age classes to look at all the relevant objectives and choose those that most suited the needs of their particular class. The ways the project teachers opted to use the objectives were varied. In fact, there were nearly as many variations as there were classes. This was partly due to it being the first year of implementation as it was felt some children needed to catch up to get to where the NLS expected them to be.

By the end of the first year, many teachers showed they had moved on from a more mechanistic approach to planning to one that took account of the needs of the children in the class. Their reflections on planning and the use of objectives were the aspects that seven of them chose as the most important thing to pass on to other teachers of mixed-age classes. Mrs Clark said 'Keep it simple' and Mrs Freeman who had a three year group class said 'Don't try and fit too much in at one go. Don't try and pick out from all three sets of objectives. . . . Because if you have too many objectives in a lesson you just lose it . . . . Limit yourself and do that well' (interview, July 1999).

Those teachers who were concerned about the difficulty of planning seemed to be those who saw the objectives as finite units to be covered as opposed to those who were able to take a more holistic stance. This can be exemplified by the way different teachers spoke about the problem. Mrs David said,

> I can see the benefits of the structure. It takes away a lot of work that the teacher has got a structure in front of them and they know where the natural progression is after covering one thing. Though it's cut down a lot of planning work and, if I had a one year group class, I think it would be very helpful. But having tried to do it with four year

groups, it's a bit of a frustrating task really. You feel, well I feel that I've not really managed to do it properly because I'm trying to do so many things at once.

(Interview, July 1999)

On the other hand, Mrs Harman who had three and, for some of the year, four year groups was enthusiastic about how well she found it worked with the mixed-age class. However, she emphasised that this was not without the cost of a huge amount of work in the planning and preparation. When asked how she found the literacy hour worked in mixed-age classes, she explained how she based her planning about the text type and grouped the objectives accordingly. She aimed high in the whole class session and then addressed the year group objectives more specifically in the independent work.

Well, it's amazingly good, I think. The planning I find absolutely horrendous and I'm not at all confident that I do it right. . . . I go back to the objectives and try and fit them in together and I do think you've got to aim high generally speaking and allow them to make allowances for the younger ones as well, as much as you can. . . . [I go] through the objectives and [try] to cover the work both in the class situation but particularly in the group work. So the group work's particularly adapted to covering the objectives. I sort of do it in the whole class and then its broken up using the objectives for each year group.

I highlight all the poetry and all the non-fiction and all the stories and then I sort of try and pick out the common theme so that I can, when using the texts, I can think of, for instance, humorous verse or verse with a rhyme or playing with language might all fit in together and I try and merge them as far as . . .

(Interview, July 1999)

Here, as was emphasised in the research described previously, flexibility is important. Also, it seems that, given the nature of the NLS, a good understanding of the subject and how the objectives relate to each other is crucial.

Differentiation

Differentiation is clearly of importance in mixed-age classes, even more so than in single-age groups. However, it is not something that was not a concern before the NLS. Catering for the differing needs of a range of abilities, age groups and learning styles is a challenge that all teachers have to address. Some of the project teachers argued at the beginning of the year that they were particularly well prepared to address this as they were well used to mixed ability teaching.

At the beginning of the year, most teachers described how they would plan different work for the different age or ability groups. In contrast, at the end of the first year, questioning was the main strategy they said they used. Some also referred to setting different tasks in the independent work time. Mrs King described how she used questioning in the literacy hour to cater for different needs.

> sometimes I'll specifically aim it at specific children and then other times it will be open to any of them so I can assess who. . . . It doesn't mean that if a year one knows a question that I'm asking to a year two it doesn't mean that they're not able to contribute as well.
>
> (Interview, July 1999)

By the end of the year, whilst acknowledging that stretching the most able and supporting those who were struggling was one of the most difficult aspects of the NLS approach, they had developed strategies for dealing with the problem. Teachers suggested a range of strategies that they found to be helpful. Looking at these closely, it appears that some are more likely than others to support children's learning in an appropriate way. Some ideas seemed more designed to help the teacher than the child. The following strategies are likely to have helped cater for differing needs in the literacy hour:

- Using carefully targeted questioning in the whole class sessions – one teacher emphasised that she planned her questions beforehand to ensure differentiation.
- Extending older or more able children by asking them to evaluate the responses given by other children.
- Setting short individual challenges in the word level session.
- Planning independent work to meet the individual need.
- Using the learning support assistant to support some groups of children (but . . . see below).
- Setting some groups of children by making, for example, three groups from two classes and employing an extra teacher.
- Planning guided work so that more experienced/older children were set off on more extended or challenging work early in the week.

More problematic were some ideas that seemed less likely to meet the learning needs of the child than the organisational needs of the teacher:

- Lowering expectations of some children, e.g. in choice of texts.
- Using the learning support assistant to help less able groups. This sometimes resulted in less challenging work being achieved.
- Setting where the least able were sent to a lower class to work with a learning support assistant on completely different tasks.

Choice of texts and pupil engagement

Choice of texts seemed to be more important for teachers of mixed-age classes than choice of objectives. Six teachers chose this as the most important thing to pass on. Mr Leonard, a Key Stage 2 teacher with three year groups in his class said,

> The best way of coping is to try and have a real variety of texts and levels of activities so that at some time you're doing a text that is really challenging the oldest group, and you're giving lots of support to the others. And other times you're giving them a fairly easy text but you're trying to think of some extension kind of activity for the older ones rather than trying to stick with the middle of the road which ends up not being terribly satisfactory for anybody really.
>
> (Interview, July 1999)

At Key Stage 1, Mrs Harman said,

> Using the books, the big books . . . it's real books, good books by proper authors with lovely language and lovely illustrations. I think that is one of the greatest aspects of the literacy hour just the enthusiasm for the book, to pass on the love of reading I think.
>
> (Interview, July 1999)

In fact, this seems to tie in with another piece of advice that teachers gave: that it is very important to make sure all children are engaged. Although on the surface this seems to be no more relevant to mixed-age classes than it is to single-age groups, there is greater potential for lack of engagement when you can have children aged from 4 to 7 years old in the same class or from 7 to 11. Mrs James, who had a year 5 and 6 class, expressed it in this way:

> An awareness that you're keeping all the children interested, that you have to be aware whether you are losing any of them basically, that's what I feel. You have to . . . Pitch it at all levels which is a silly thing to say, but you have to make sure that they're all getting something from it particularly. . . . When you're doing your whole class bit and the plenary, that they're all getting something back from it.
>
> (Interview, July 1999)

As Mrs Odgers, who had all of Key Stage 1 in her class, explained, 'Choose the big books carefully, so that the children are all going to enjoy them and get something from them . . . you do need to find some way of engaging them all in the shared work' (interview, July 1999). Most teachers picked out the shared text work as the part they liked best in the literacy hour, stressing their and the children's enjoyment of the texts. The section on shared reading in the Framework of Objectives underlines the potential of this for scaffolded learning.

> At both key stages, because the teacher is supporting the reading, pupils can work from texts that are beyond their independent reading levels. This is particularly valuable for less able readers who gain access to texts of greater richness and complexity than they would otherwise be able to read. This builds confidence and teaches more advanced skills which feed into other independent reading.
>
> (DfEE, 1998: 11)

Four factors emerge from this that seem important to successful differentiation in the literacy hour when planning for a substantial part of the literacy teaching is based on texts:

1 The texts chosen should be of high quality and be challenging.
2 Teachers need to plan for how they intend to engage the wide range of abilities in the reading and understanding of the texts.
3 Key teaching points need to be reinforced for the different age groups through questioning and appropriate activities.
4 Further reading and appropriate extension activities need to be provided for the most able, older children to make sure they are adequately challenged.

Flexibility

Flexibility is a word that has recurred in this study. Research into small schools has emphasised the importance of flexibility in teaching mixed-age classes (Bell and Sigsworth, 1987; Hopkins and Ellis, 1991; Vulliamy and Webb, 1995; Harber, 1996). Advice to teachers in small schools on the introduction of the NLS from an LEA with a large number of small schools said,

> By their very nature, small schools are used to providing for differentiation and tailoring their curriculum to meet the fluctuating demands of classes from year to year. It is this need for flexibility and differentiation, hallmarks of good practice in small schools, which has enabled them to respond so successfully to the demands of the NLP. Indeed, evidence from Norfolk has demonstrated that small schools within the county were better able to adapt to meet the requirements of the Framework than larger schools with more rigid curriculum structures.
>
> Undeniably, the introduction of the National Literacy Strategy does raise singular challenges for small schools, particularly with regard to issues of planning and resourcing. Crucially it is important that schools

do not look upon the framework as providing a straightjacket. Rather they should view it as a supportive structure within which teachers can be creative, using their professional judgement to provide a stimulating appropriately focused approach to the teaching of literacy.

(Devon Curriculum Services, 1998)

Despite this and other similar advice from other LEAs, in the early days of the NLS, the apparent rigidity of the structure caused concern to many teachers, not just those in small schools. Over the two years of the study, there was more encouragement from NLS consultants and through published guidelines for teachers to use their professional judgement in how they implemented the NLS.

The feeling of restriction was evident in interviews with teachers at the end of the first year. Twelve of the twenty teachers mentioned frustration with the time restrictions. For some people this was just irritation with particular time slots as being too long or too short. There was also a sense that what one teacher described as the 'relentless' pace meant there was no space for spontaneity or even time to review. By the end of the second year, there was much more a feeling that they were able to rediscover their professional expertise and adapt the literacy hour to fit their needs.

As was seen above, those teachers who adopted a flexible approach to planning found the framework of objectives easier to work with. At the end of the first year, two teachers chose this as the most important piece of advice to pass on. Mrs Ibbotsen a Key Stage 1 teacher said,

> not to get too bogged down in it. Go back to your professional judgement and you have to have faith in what you are doing and go with it. Use your expertise to change it around and link it in . . . be flexible in your approach.
>
> (Interview, July 1999)

This sense of ownership was much more in evidence after two years of the strategy. The comments from many of the sixty-one teachers who responded to the questionnaire in July 2000, reflected this in response to the question 'Which aspects of the NLS do you feel most positive about?'

> 'Ability now to develop what we think is best for our children' (head teacher, teaching year 5 and year 6).
> 'I feel the theory behind the literacy strategy is very useful. As long as you can organise the format for the benefit of your own pupils and your school' (class teacher, reception and year 1).
> 'Having a structure to what needs to be learned/taught is helpful but we do not use it as a straightjacket' (class teacher, year 1 and year 2).

Three teachers commented negatively on the rigidity of the framework. One of these said, 'We are extremely flexible about it!' and another said they would be doing things differently next year. Only one showed a sense of powerlessness to adapt the NLS to suit their needs.

The interviews with the project teachers who were visited at the end of the second year also reflect this sense that they had regained control over their teaching. Mrs Freeman said she felt more confident in what she was doing now that she knew the Framework better and was therefore more able to match the NLS to her class and individual children.

These teachers were also able to talk about how they were adapting their planning to suit the mixed-age class. Mrs York had reorganised the text types in different terms so that they fitted the year groups she was teaching. Mrs Milne (teaching years 3 to 6) did guided writing with her oldest group early in the week so that they could start and move on quickly, whereas she worked with younger children later in the week as she felt this was when they needed most support. Mrs Quick, in particular, emphasised the need for flexibility and said how she felt her teaching had improved now she was being more flexible.

Catering for the youngest children

Chapter 9 focuses on the needs of the youngest children in school but it is worth noting here that meeting the needs of these children seems to be one area of the NLS that the project teachers were not happy about. After two years of the NLS, the interviews show that most teachers felt that there had been real changes in the way they approached literacy teaching, and for the most part these teachers seemed happy about this. However, four of the six Key Stage 1 teachers interviewed questioned the suitability of the literacy strategy for the youngest children. Mrs Noakes said she felt the freedom of the child had been taken away, 'but' she added, 'they cope'. Mrs Channing was finding it very hard to find suitable independent activities for the youngest children and was dissatisfied with just a diet of worksheets but found the most useful activities required an adult to be with them. Although Mrs Harman felt her teaching of writing had improved, she felt the youngest children were inhibited in their use of emergent writing.

Mrs King was particularly aware of the needs of young children. The advice she wanted to pass on to other teachers of mixed-age classes was

> I think definitely trying to hold onto the practical side or creating play based practical activities for reception especially. And trying to do that within a mixed-age class is quite hard really unless you've got class-room support but I think that's definitely the most important – not that I do it well.
>
> (Interview, July 1999)

To set against this, these teachers also reflected on how the youngest children seemed to enjoy picking up and trying out skills that they had heard being taught to older year groups. This is described in the next chapter.

Summary

Despite our concerns before the implementation of the NLS, neither the teachers who responded to the questionnaire nor the teachers in the project felt the NLS was entirely unsuitable for mixed-age classes. Those who did find it most difficult were those who had four age groups in their class. Teachers with only two year groups felt it worked well. This was reflected in some way by our observations of children's progress. There was no difference in levels of engagement of target children in classes with more year groups.

Teachers found that it was not advisable to try to cover several objectives to reflect the different year groups in the class. They preferred to keep their teaching focused and to try to group similar objectives and text types together in some way. There was a large degree of agreement that it is important to be flexible in planning and teaching the NLS in mixed-age classes. Many of the teachers had moved from differentiating mostly by setting different group activities to using questioning to reinforce or extend children's thinking. They still took different abilities and age into account when planning for group work, both guided and independent.

Many teachers felt strongly that having high expectations of what children can do was important. They reported that younger children enjoyed trying out things they had seen older children learning. They particularly felt that good quality texts were important. Despite initial misgivings they found younger and less able children benefited from enjoying challenging and high quality texts.

The main concern about the literacy hour with mixed-age classes was for the youngest children in school. Teachers with reception children in the same class as year 1 and even year 2 children found it difficult to cater adequately for their needs. They found it difficult to plan for appropriate play-based activities and that work sheets could easily become a quick but unsatisfactory option. Despite this, some teachers reported their surprise at how children learned to sit still for half an hour and cope with the increased pace of learning.

Advice for teachers of mixed-age classes

The study of these twenty teachers in classes containing two to four year groups points above all to flexibility. This reflects research findings from other studies into teaching in small schools before the introduction of the literacy hour. This research also indicates that, although it may be difficult to teach four year groups in one class, it is certainly possible to do it well and successfully. Both from our observations and the teachers' own advice the following points seem to be important:

- Knowing the subject and the framework allows teachers to group related objectives together so that teaching can be focused as well as covering relevant objectives. The map of development provided by the framework supports teachers in this.

- Having different age groups in one class does not mean that teaching and learning activities need to be fragmented to meet different needs. Having high expectations of children and actively supporting and/or challenging individuals leads to an appropriate experience for children even when ages differ considerably.
- Good quality texts can provide the key to motivating children with a range of different abilities.
- There are many positive benefits in learning in a mixed-age group. Teachers would do well to plan to capitalise on these benefits through co-operative and collaborative work.
- The youngest children in school need to be planned for with plenty of play and exploratory activities. Independent work does not have to mean filling in worksheets: open-ended activities encourage children to learn to operate independently.

9 Four-year-olds and the literacy hour

Introduction

This chapter focuses on the youngest children in school and how those in the project schools fared in the literacy hour. The issue of the 4-year-old in school is one that has long given rise to concern (DES, 1990; Sharp *et al.*, 1994). Recently, questions have been raised about the suitability of the literacy hour for the youngest children in school (Fisher, 2000). The NLS requires all children from age 4 to 11 to be taught a literacy hour each day. Even where extra guidance was produced for teachers of 4-year-olds the emphasis is on preparation for the literacy hour rather than encouraging developmentally appropriate practice, 'Teachers should plan to introduce a full literacy hour as soon as possible and, at the very latest, by the end of the term before children move into Year 1' (i.e. 5 years of age) (DfEE, 1998: 103). This is despite the recognition of early years educators that, 'the younger children are the more vital it is that they are offered a curriculum which responds to their developmental needs' (Hurst, 1997: 14).

This concern is particularly acute in mixed-age classes where children from 4 to 6 or 7 are taught together. In the past, whether these children have been planned for separately or included with other year groups depended on the suitability of the activities, the amount of classroom support, the resources available and the number of 4-year-olds in a given year. However, within the literacy hour, the NLS sets out discrete objectives for children in the Foundation Stage that must either be integrated with the more advanced objectives or addressed separately. Problems arise as the objectives for year 1 and year 2 may be developmentally inappropriate for the youngest children in the class. Therefore, how the reception children spend their time during the literacy hour depends to a great extent on the way the teacher interprets the NLS and what resources are made available. The NLS, with its age-related objectives but universal literacy hour format, brings this to light as an important issue for all early years practitioners.

Teachers' and 4-year-olds' responses to the NLS

There were forty-five reception age children in eight of the ten Key Stage 1 classes at the start of the year. The number increased during the year after a new intake started in January. The inclusion of the reception children in the mixed-age classes meant that they shared the time and attention of their teacher with year 1 children in four classes, with year 1 and 2 children in three classes, and in one case with years 1, 2 and 3. This was either directly in whole class sessions or indirectly through work planned by the teacher but delivered by someone else. The proportion of reception children to older children in these classes was as small as one to fifteen and as large as fourteen to ten. Although class composition and ratios were different each term as new children came into the class, teachers had to address the needs of each year group.

Teachers' responses in the initial interviews were mainly positive about the NLS and only three raised concern about providing for 4-year-olds at the same time as 5-, 6- and even 7-year olds all together in a literacy hour. This seemed to be rationalised by the acknowledgement that a single year group class can have as much as a 5-year ability range anyway and the fact that teachers in mixed-age classes have always had to cater for this range of individual needs. There were no direct questions in the initial interview for the project relating to the youngest children, however, the teachers were asked for ways that they organised their teaching and classroom for their mixed-age class prior to the NLS. Most of the teachers had organised their teaching around group teaching with many using some whole class sessions mainly for introducing activities. In fact, the system of introducing a topic with the children on the carpet followed by group work was a common format. Teachers acknowledged that the NLS brought new focus and more structure to their literacy lessons. Of the eight Key Stage 1 teachers with 4-year-olds, three spontaneously mentioned them in the first interview as an issue.

> 'My concern about it is with the little children . . . I think they should have thought more carefully about the younger children' (Mrs Ibbotsen, interview, September 1998).
> 'The hardest thing is knowing the difference between the nursery section the year ones and twos and trying to incorporate all the things that you think you should be spending time on' (Mrs King, interview September 1998).
> 'They're little, they're forty-eight months old. They're four years old, you know!' (Mrs Clark, interview, September 1998).

By the end of the summer term the Key Stage 1 teachers were even more positive about the NLS, claiming to have secured more insight and more confidence over the year. They felt that their subject knowledge was much improved, as was the quality of their teaching. They were also able to point to changes and improvements in the children's learning and the 4-year-olds were mentioned more often as a separate group with separate needs. At this stage some additional questions on the 4-year-olds were included in the interview. These highlighted particular issues such as how reception was managed and what activities the teacher considered to be appropriate.

Two factors from the first year that helped build positive perceptions of the literacy hour were the use of big books and children's response. These aspects were not exclusively related to the 4-year-olds but they undoubtedly influenced the development of the youngest children's literacy. First, new resources including big books were greatly appreciated and enjoyed by all. In fact some Key Stage 1 teachers felt the big books were really the key to a successful literacy hour. They were attractive and appealing to the children with good texts from which the objectives could be taught.

> they are encouraged to enjoy the book. I love that; and I love the way that the work comes from the book in context. If you're doing word work you can pick it out from the text, if you're doing sentences you can pick them out from the text. It's not out of context.
>
> (Mrs Harman, interview, July 1999)

Second, teachers said all the children regardless of age responded well to work in the literacy hour. Mrs King said children were 'increasingly able to communicate their understanding and use appropriate terminology. They were curious about language and they loved the text-level work' (interview, July 1999).

However, alongside the positive feelings and more specifically related to 4-year-olds, were their reservations about incorporating the youngest children into the literacy hour. Mrs Ibbotsen argued, 'I think reception should be a separate class altogether . . . I don't think it's [the literacy hour] really appropriate for 5- and 6-year-olds but certainly not 4-year-olds' (interview, July 1999).

Despite teachers' comments that children responded well in the literacy hour and teachers' efforts to include the 4-year-olds in the whole class sections, the objectives being taught were often in advance of their experience. Not surprisingly the youngest children were often observed fiddling and fidgeting. When required to sit quietly for a length of time they were sometimes seen as restless, tired, confused or staring into space. When not actively engaged while on the carpet, the reception children might play with hair, socks, shoes, suck their thumbs, bite their fingernails and could be disruptive. In the guided time they sometimes (as 4-year-olds do) appeared to lack concentration and occasionally refused to do the independent task that was asked of them. The literacy hour did not always seem an interesting and involving time for the 4-year-olds. This is important to note as it may indicate that some aspects of the literacy hour may be inappropriate for these children. If not fully involved and appropriately catered for, these children may find it difficult to settle into school or even become disaffected from literacy learning. Mrs Smith echoed this in the end of year interview, 'What I tend to do is spend half the time asking them to sit nicely maybe that's because they're so young, but they're tired at that point' (interview, July 1999).

Observation of 4-year-olds in the literacy hour

These impressions were not uniform across all classes. Observations of the 4-year-old target children showed them to be often attentive and contributing to the literacy hour as well as the instances where they were fidgeting and inattentive. In studying the observational data for the project where it relates to the reception children as a group, it appeared that some children were more able to participate in the activities in each segment of the hour and seemed to be more settled into the expectations of the classroom. There were some classes where these children seemed to be actively engaged in the hour and others where children's behaviour indicated less engagement with the lesson.

A more detailed and in-depth study of the 4-year-olds was not the main aim of the project, however, in terms of attention, engagement and participation, the observational data give an indication of children's involvement during the literacy hour. Teachers adopted a range of approaches to involving 4-year-olds. Examples of these are given in Figure 9.1. Here,

---

ATTITUDE TO THE LITERACY HOUR

- Children join in only those parts of the literacy hour that the teacher thinks will be meaningful to them. This has included some whole class sections, e.g. shared text work and the plenary although not for every literacy hour. The teacher uses the teaching assistant to provide alternative activities for the 4-year-olds at other times.
- On the other hand, from the time of the children's induction to school they take part in the entire literacy format because the teacher says that to do otherwise 'will give them the wrong idea of school' and they 'have to get used to it anyway'.

LITERACY SKILLS

- The teacher encourages and supports the children's emergent skills. She also teaches reading and writing strategies like using pictures for clues, reading over an unknown word, sounding out words, using a high frequency work bank, checking to see if it makes sense; and reminds the children regularly to use them as aids for growing independence.
- On the other hand, the teacher acknowledges that children sometimes write emergently, however she prioritises phonic skills and the use of word cards to support writing. She helps children individually when they request it.

(Continued over)

(Continued)

SHARED TEXT WORK

- The children's spontaneous comments are accepted, answered and extended when appropriate. The children are encouraged to think and express their opinions as well as reflect upon their own experiences and share with others.
- On the other hand, the teacher focuses on the task at hand, e.g. generating rhyming words or reading a text in order to identify who the characters are. The teacher asks specific closed questions. The teacher interacts with the children only to explain things they get wrong or don't understand or to address behaviour.

WORD/SENTENCE WORK

- Phonics are drawn out through the context of the shared story/text or lesson. For example, the children made up a collaborative story where everyone contributed one sentence. When the story was finished, the teacher wrote one of the sentences on the board asking the children to help her spell/sound out the words.
- On the other hand, the teacher used prepared sheets with rhyming word or CVC word exercises requiring answers to be filled in. The words are not linked with the text.

INDEPENDENT AND GUIDED GROUP TASKS

- Children are asked to write their own stories, rhymes, etc using their emergent writing strategies.
- Children take part in open-ended activities with the teacher supporting their use of literacy stategies, e.g. sounding out words. Teacher uses the child's efforts as an assessment for what is presently being achieved and to give an idea of the next likely challenge.
- Children explore literacy behaviour through playing with writing materials, puppets etc.
- On the other hand, children are given worksheets with tasks that stem from the phonic word work. Four-year-olds dictate sentences, which the teaching assistant writes for them to trace over and then copy.
- Or, children sometimes misinterpret what the teacher has asked them to do or once they've gone to their table have forgotten what to do. When asked, children can't explain what they are doing or say they don't know what they are doing. They sometimes can't read the words they are writing.

PLENARY

- The teacher notices the cognitive content of the children's contributions, validates and sometimes extends ideas through questions. The focus is on making links between personal experience and literacy skills. Objectives covered in the lesson are reinforced.
- On the other hand the main focus is on good behaviour and correct answers. The teacher uses controlling language like 'I will get cross if you don't sit nicely'.

Figure 9.1   Examples of differences in approach to involvement of 4-year-olds in the literacy hour.

different approaches to the education of young children can be discerned. These differences are neither new nor peculiar to the NLS, however, they may well impact on these children's attitudes and achievement. Some teachers seem to be concerned to provide appropriate experiences whereas others are more concerned to prepare children for the next stage in their development.

Advice for teachers of reception children was limited in the early stages of the implementation of the NLS. It was only after the first year that more detailed advice was given, for example,

> *Planning for reception classes.* Planning for reception needs to reflect the different experiences and development levels of children. The very different levels of understanding will require teachers to plan carefully pitched class teaching and group activities. It is important to use such focused group and shared time to support children towards the appropriate whole class objectives.
>
> (DfEE, 2000b: 4)

Play and activities for the 4-year-olds during the literacy hour

The research described in this book focused exclusively on children and teachers' experiences in the literacy hour. We had no observational data and only passing reference in the interviews to what other planned literacy activities went on in the rest of the day. While we have some questions about much of the experience provided for 4-year-olds in the literacy hour, we have no evidence that this was not counter-balanced by what happened in the remaining hours of the day.

In the initial set of interviews before the implementation of the NLS, teachers did not bring up concerns about the importance role play has for young children in literacy learning. This may have been because of the strong emphasis in the NLS on direct and focused teaching of literacy objectives. It is equally important to note, however, that there were no specific interview questions to prompt the teachers to comment on the role of play in literacy. Teachers seemed to be focused on the teaching aspects of the literacy curriculum rather than observing children's developing literacy behaviours in play situations. Some teachers also expressed a wariness of play during the literacy hour. If the reception children were seen to be playing, the older children might be distracted from their more formal work.

The observations showed that most of the Key Stage 1 literacy hour sessions during the project included the 4-year-olds in the whole class sessions. Two of the teachers however limited the whole class input to the shared reading/writing only; following this the 4-year-olds would go off with the teaching assistant for the rest of the session. This was explained in two ways. First, that the 4-year-olds could take part in appropriate age-

related activities in a small group. Second, the teacher was free to concentrate on teaching the older children. Eight of the nine classes had the help of a teaching assistant who worked exclusively with the 4-year-olds. When the teaching assistant was absent, then the teacher would work with those children. This was a regular pattern that raises questions about the roles of the adults. Is it correct that objectives to be taught to the older children always require and deserve the expertise of the teacher, whereas untrained adults can adequately meet the needs of the 4-year-olds? In the one class that did not have the support of a teaching assistant, the teacher worked with the 4-year-olds while the older children got on with independent work. When the reception children were settled, she would move around the groups to check on progress. This was, however, as stated by the teacher, a choice of expediency than of pedagogy. Reception children worked independently during the guided/individual time only occasionally when there were no alternatives. These observations of the literacy hour present glimpses of the complexity of the decisions required by teachers and raise the question of what is best for both the older children and the younger children in the same class.

A range of activities was provided for the 4-year-olds during the guided/ independent time of the literacy hour sometimes when the children were with the teaching assistant, sometimes when working independently. From the observations six categories were generated that described typical sorts of things the 4-year-olds took part in during this 20-minute section of the literacy hour. They included:

- *Adult led pencil and paper tasks* – usually things like practising letter formation, emergent writing, tracing over highlighter pen or copying words written by an adult, also worksheets and colouring.
- *Adult initiated playful tasks (done with an adult)* – these were things like a Feely Box, word games, puppets, practical activities, role-play, drawing pictures.
- *Reading* – this included reading individually, guided reading and talking about the illustrations in a picture book.
- *Watching TV* – this was 'Words and Pictures'.
- *Computer* – packages like 'My Alphabet' and 'Tizzy's Toybox'.
- *Play activities* such as playdough, Roll & Write, pegboards, word games. Teachers described these as 'holding activities' when there was no adult available.

For most of the classes pencil and paper tasks were the most frequent activities used in the guided/independent time. Every teacher also provided 'playful tasks' such as drawing pictures and word games and less frequently, practical activities or role-play, dance or drama. Particular teachers and teaching assistants chose to use TV and the computer on a regular basis; and activities such as reading and play as a holding activity were used to a lesser degree by many. The children appeared to enjoy many of the activities provided in this part of the literacy hour as well as the opportunities within them to talk to their friends and the teaching assistant.

By the end of the year the needs of the reception children within the literacy hour were more apparent to the teachers. In the second interview teachers mentioned the difficulty of providing for play at the same time as catering for older children. Mrs Ibbotsen gives an insight into the teachers' perspective on play and the literacy hour at this time:

> I still really believe in that [child-centred education] but I don't think it's as appropriate in present day circumstances because the literacy hour knocks that one on the head for a start . . . you get this feeling when the literacy was presented that it [play] mustn't be, it is language it's not you know something else in disguise.
>
> (Mrs Ibbotsen, interview, July 1999)

Management of 4-year-olds in the literacy hour

From the point of view of the Key Stage 1 teachers the management of the literacy hour was problematic. The differing capabilities of the range of children in the class made catering for the needs of all children difficult. In these classes there were children who were writing stories independently alongside children who were just beginning to learn their sounds. As stated before, eight of the nine teachers had regular teaching assistant support during the literacy hour and in most cases the reception children were removed during part of the hour to work with the teaching assistant. The teachers increasingly over the year expressed a desire to provide appropriate play-based activities for the reception children and felt that it was essential to have the support of a teaching assistant during the hour for this purpose. 'I have been able to adapt it for the reception children and I'm lucky enough to have a teaching assistant who will go off and do these wonderful things . . . making puppets . . . environmental print . . . role play' (Mrs Freeman, interview, July 1999).

Teachers seemed to believe that if they had a teaching assistant the 4-year-olds would be appropriately provided for. The children would be supplied with 'wonderful' activities for their age away from the formal demands of the literacy hour. However, in practice, the most common activities observed for 4-year-olds during the guided/independent time were adult-led pencil and paper tasks. In the majority of cases this was tracing or copy-writing and in some instances the adult guided the child's hand in very focused writing tasks. Mark making, emergent writing or writing for real-life purposes were noticeably absent during most literacy hours as were role-play and child initiated or other exploratory writing activities. More play-based activities may have occurred during other times in the day but few were observed during the literacy hour. It was also observed that children sometimes went from sitting on the carpet with the teacher to sitting at a table with a teaching assistant for the remainder of the hour. These methods perhaps stem from the directive for 100 per cent direct teaching time during the literacy hour, or from the notion that children in the literacy hour should be sitting in their seats with a pencil in their hand, or from the fear that any more active behaviour the younger children display will cause the older ones to stray from their work.

Present circumstances of an increasing number of 4-year-olds in reception classes, a literacy hour designed as a formal, structured lesson and evidence (e.g. Barrett, 1989) claiming that young children can be disaffected from school with too much too soon require teachers to consider how best to involve 4-year-olds in literacy learning. The management of 4-year-olds during the literacy hour, brings up the question of how the teacher interprets the requirements of the literacy hour in the light of good early years practice and the Early Learning Goals (QCA, 1999). There are benefits in planning the literacy hour with the collaboration of other adults so that the needs of all the children can be considered and addressed with flexibility. However, the use of these other adults has to be questioned. Only rarely were they used to develop independent learning or to increase opportunities for interaction between adults and the youngest children. More frequently their function seemed to reduce children's ability to make their own choices or engage in more open-ended activities.

Learning from older children

Teachers seemed aware of the rich possibilities inherent in children rubbing shoulders with their elders and commented on the positive instances where the younger children learned in the shadow of the older ones in mixed-age classes. Mrs Noakes commented on how children had picked up on the use of punctuation marks and terms such as 'illustrator' and 'author'. 'They're just picking it up from the year ones and from the group session. So I think it must be beneficial' (interview, July 1999).

However, generally, the benefits for the 4-year-olds from being in a mixed-age class seemed to have been viewed as no more than a lucky spin-off of the literacy hour. That is, the awareness of the younger children learning from the models the older children presented in whole class sessions did not develop into capitalising on that potential in the independent work. There were no strategies for children of mixed ages to work together during the hour unless they were of the same ability. Teachers who advocated collaborative work planned for it to occur within age groups not across them. Peer tutoring or buddy systems across ages were not evident during the literacy hour. However, this can hardly be surprising given that the NLS was designed to be taught according to year groups.

One instance in which children were observed to mix was the free reading time, which happened in some of the schools immediately after the literacy hour. Here children of all ages were seen sharing books, reading or pretend reading, engaged in discussion about the pictures or story, sitting companionably or with arms thrown around each other creating the positive atmosphere that is likely to promote conditions that facilitate learning. Children were free to make connections with all ages, the younger ones benefiting from more experienced guidance and older ones taking responsibility and consolidating their knowledge. These are the kind of rich encounters that single-age classes miss out on and that the promotion of age-based teaching objectives discourages. However, after two years of the project, these types of activities had been introduced and developed in some of the project schools, for example, peer tutoring and paired reading.

Differentiation

'The Literacy Hour offers a structure of classroom management, designed to maximise the time teachers spend directly teaching their class' (DfEE, 1998: 10). Instead of giving each child a little individual attention, this approach advocates sharing the teacher's expertise with the whole class for much of the lesson. This supports the notion that this maximises the potential of the teacher's time and that both extremes in ability will benefit either through extension or consolidation according to the child's needs; and that high expectations will be held for all. A whole class approach, however, does not negate the need for the teacher to be aware of and provide for individual children's needs or strategies to promote progress. The Key Stage 1 teachers on the project were well aware at the start of the project of the need to differentiate various aspects of their teaching in order to meet the needs of all their children.

> There's a lot of differentiation . . . I have to plan for my reception, my year ones, but it's not as easy as that because some of my brighter reception have overtaken my lower year ones, so basically I'm planning for the individual child. . . . You assess where they are and plan from there onwards, but it's usually ends up in about three groups per lesson.
>
> (Mrs Clark, interview, September 1998)

This small sample of Key Stage 1 teachers had various ways of differentiating for the wide range of ability, which included the 4-year-olds in their classes. For example, most of the teachers said that they differentiated through their questioning. In practice, this was exhibited during the whole class shared sections of the literacy hour. Their questioning showed that they were aware of an individual child's abilities. For example, Mrs Noakes asked the reception children to spell 'the', 'it', 'had' as opposed to 'animals', 'quarrel', etc., for year 1; or reception children were asked to find a full stop and capital letter, whereas year 1 children were asked to find words with apostrophes.

Not surprisingly, whether the newest children were sitting quietly, listening and watching or distracted in some way, if the teacher asked them a question directly more often than not the child would have an answer and respond. In this way teachers endeavoured to involve them actively in the lesson. This is important given that the teachers aimed the shared work to the year 1 or year 2 objectives, not reception. Also, as in any class, it can take some time for new children to feel confident enough to join in. Therefore, the teacher's high expectations and facilitation helped the reception children not only to be involved in the literacy hour but also to be integrated into the class.

Other ways in which the teachers differentiated for 4-year-olds are outlined below:

- Through the use of classroom support. For example, if a teacher had the support of a teaching assistant, the 4-year-olds worked with her during the guided/independent time.
- Activities were designed for children's abilities and interests. For example, after reading a poem 'Bears': reception made chairs for toy bears using Duplo, year 1 made rhyming badges for the bears, another year 1 group wrote a similar poem using sentence starters, year made a list of rhyming words and wrote a poem.
- The length of time the reception children remained in the whole class session and to what degree they were expected to work independently varied. In the majority of classes the 4-year-old children sat on the carpet for the first half of the literacy hour. Occasionally, if no adults were available, 4-year-olds worked independently, but would be checked on regularly by the teacher.
- Through the kind of involvement the 4-year-olds had in the activities in the whole class session, i.e. were they fun, involving and inclusive? In some instances the youngest children were asked questions regularly and posed challenges.
- The role of phonics: the younger children as might be expected, focused much more on the learning of initial sounds than the older children. This was reinforced in work with the teaching assistant and in the activities done in the guided time.

Pace

The pace of the literacy lesson has been determined to be an important part of being effective in teaching literacy. Pace is defined by the NLS as being brisk and business-like, i.e. 'there is a sense of urgency, driven by the need to make progress and succeed' (DfEE, 1998: 8). However, in the Key Stage 1 classes observed, the teachers' use of pace seemed to be linked more with purposefulness of the lesson.

> pace seems well suited to the children teacher appears to have clear objectives in mind and well thought out strategies to help her on her way to meeting them. I would call her pace sure and steady rather than brisk and business like
>
> (Mrs King, observation, July 1999)

> teacher seems to be constantly creating opportunities in which children have the chance to succeed. This seems to come from her detailed knowledge of each child and her belief that their self-esteem is important for their learning. There is no sense of a driving pace but there is a great sense of purpose in teacher's approach
>
> (Mrs Noakes, observation, May 1999)

When asked explicitly in the follow-up interview whether the literacy hour had altered their pace of teaching, teachers referred more to content coverage than speed or progress through a lesson and there was only one reference to clock watching. This seems to reflect their growing awareness of many more aspects of literacy content and their increased subject knowledge. Mrs Channing said, 'we do get through quite a lot in that time', and Mrs Ibbotsen said, 'It's changed the pace I think in that you are trying to hit a lot of areas within say a term's planning'. But in relation to the 4-year-olds she said 'I don't feel they have enough time perhaps to just sit and talk and talk about them[selves] and what they are doing and how it relates to them. Snap, snap snap [the way the literacy hour goes]' (interviews, July 1999).

It seems that it is through knowing the individual children that the teachers found the correct pace for the lesson. After two years of the NLS, teachers were more relaxed about the pace of progression. As teachers of mixed-age classes they said they were less worried about coverage than they had been. They had realised that having children for more than one year meant that younger children could meet objectives again in the following year. Teachers also became more relaxed about the timing of the hour and thus more able to react to children's responses.

Self-esteem

The first year of formal schooling is important in that it establishes a child's attitude to school and learning. If they are happy and motivated to learn because they find it enjoyable and useful and it gives them power and confidence then, children are more likely to be well disposed to learn to read and write and speak and listen. The link between the language the teacher uses in the classroom and the child's disposition to learn is perhaps obvious but some teachers seemed better able to nurture this than others. For example, Mrs Noakes often illustrated literacy as an interesting, enjoyable and useful part of children's lives. She celebrated the youngest children's contributions. For instance when a child noticed part of her friend's name in another word she called her to the front of the class to discuss it. The observer wrote, 'it seems as though the teacher tries to find a special moment or a particular success for every child . . . is respectful and supportive of the children's self-initiated tasks and growing skill' (field notes, May 1999). Her attitude and approach to children's attempts to use literacy within the literacy hour seemed to empower the children to go beyond the acquisition of a set of skills for school use only. On the other hand, other teachers sometimes had the attitude that the youngest children must be taught how to behave appropriately.

> Three (reception) children remain on the carpet to draw a picture of a clock. These are children the teacher has told me she can do nothing with. One boy has broken his pencil lead 'deliberately' says the teacher 'he's naughty and must wait'. Even though there's a big picture of a clock in the big book to refer to these boys have been positioned with their backs to the book away to the side.
>
> (Observation, June 1999)

These examples highlight the important role the teacher plays in developing children's attitude to and engagement in literacy events.

Successful teaching of 4-year-olds

It is not the intention to offer a conclusive prescription on how to be an effective teacher of the literacy hour for 4-year-olds, but to raise questions and issues to be considered when interpreting, organising for and managing the NLS for young children.

Effectiveness for 4-year-olds was judged:

- through progress made in test scores over the year, which gave a measure of reading readiness and language awareness;
- through progress made in writing as reflected in the writing samples of the target children;
- in how the children settled into being in school as reflected in the target children's response to the literacy hour, i.e. their involvement.

No claims can be made for a particular teacher's effectiveness during the project, but references to the tests, writing and behaviour are included as catalysts for thinking and discussion.

The reception children took the LARR test in the autumn at the beginning of the project. This is not a reading test but a pencil and paper test that considers the awareness the child has on concepts about print, e.g. recognising print in the environment, distinguishing between numbers and letters. All the children had made gains when they took the same test eight months later. Progress of target children, i.e. one from each school who had an average score on the first test, ranged from 4 points to 23 points shown on the second test. This indicates that the children had gained knowledge about the function of print and reading and writing conventions (although it may also indicate an increased ability to sit and respond to the teacher's questions). Research has shown that knowledge of concepts of print is one important indicator of a child's progress in reading by the end of their first year of school (Riley, 1996). Shared reading and writing supports this learning.

Writing samples were collected from the target children each month. These reflected the progress individual children made in their writing according to the criteria described in Chapter 5, the aspects of writing that were focused upon and the kinds of opportunities for writing that were available during the literacy hour. Teaching writing in the first half of the literacy hour presents a departure from previous practice where children learned to write either through tracing over or copying the teacher's writing or through using their own emergent writing to express their ideas. Clearly in the former approach the teacher or an adult needs to be on hand to provide the text to be copied or traced. The latter approach where children's independent efforts are encouraged seems to be more suited to independent and guided work. In the literacy hour the teaching of writing would take place during shared writing in which the teacher models how to write, in word-level work where children are taught handwriting and spelling and in guided writing where children are taught in a group.

As was reported in Chapter 5, teachers were far less likely to do shared writing than shared reading. Indeed, of the teachers who had reception children in their class, only Mrs Smith, Mrs King, Mrs Channing and Mrs Clark wrote in front of children on a regular basis. On the other, hand children in Mrs Harman, Mrs Ibbotsen, Mrs Smith, Mrs King, Mrs Channing and Mrs Noakes' classes did do guided writing on some occasions – although not as frequently as guided reading. The content of these guided writing sessions varied from explicit teaching of word segmentation for spelling (Mrs King) to copy writing (Mrs Ibbotsen). Only Mrs Noakes seemed to use guided writing to teach children strategies for writing independently. She would set prescribed writing tasks such as using particular words from the list of high frequency words or filling in speech bubbles from the story of the *Three Little Pigs*. She provided children with a range of word banks and lists and encouraged them to find out the spelling they needed from these, if they could not they learned to put dots to replace the graphemes they did not know. This had a positive impact on children's spelling and handwriting but seemed less successful in encouraging development of personal style. Mrs Harman raised the question about children's confidence as emergent writers at the end of the second year. She said she felt that children's increased awareness of how to go about finding the correct spelling of words (through segmentation and by using word lists) had made the the youngest children inhibited in 'having a go'.

Progress in writing

The target child who had the highest progress score on the literacy awareness test was Annie in Mrs Noakes' class. By comparing her writing sample in September (Figure 9.2) with the one in July (Figure 9.3), it is clear that she has made progress in writing as well.

Over the year her handwriting has become more confident and correctly formed. She uses semi-phonetic spelling at the beginning of the year but by the second term can spell simple words correctly and makes good phonetic attempts such as 'liv'. She is using capital letters by January and full stops by March. However, her use of vocabulary remains limited and she uses mainly simple sentences. This may be as a result of the approach to teaching writing described above.

Observation of Annie's behaviour indicated that she had settled into school well. She had made friends and was taking an active part in the literacy hour. Field notes recall that Annie

> is attentive and involved . . . seems excited about the story and spontaneously makes a comment . . . spells 'pig' easily and confidently . . . talks in an animated way with the children in her group . . . speaks confidently about her drawing to teacher in front of the class
>
> (Target child observation, March 1999)

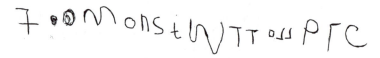

Figure 9.2   Annie's writing in September.
(The monsters went to the park)

Figure 9.3   Annie's writing in July.
(Look at Sam Look at Sam I like Sam This is Sam. This is my friend. He lives in N . . . . [local village]. He is eight.)

Summary

The literacy hour presented some problems for the teachers of the youngest children in school, particularly these teachers who had mixed-age classes. The need to provide developmentally appropriate practice for 4-year-olds at the same time as addressing the needs of 5-, 6- and even 7-year-olds was challenging. Nevertheless there were teachers who had children who seemed settled and who made good progress in literacy. The research reported here seems to indicate the following points:

- It is difficult to cater effectively for 4-year-olds in the literacy hour, particularly in mixed-age classes where the needs of the youngest children may not take priority.
- The separate sections of the literacy hour can be entirely appropriate for 4-year-olds provided the content and activities are developmentally appropriate.
- It is important to achieve children's interest and engagement in the activities through targeted questioning, children's active involvement in the lesson and the tasks and through supporting children's self-esteem.
- Independent work should be more than holding activities designed to keep children occupied while the teacher teaches other children.
- Adult help can be used to develop independence, provide enhanced opportunities for interaction and support exploratory activities. However, it can also limit the development of independence.
- Care needs to be taken to avoid letting direct teaching inhibit children's developing creativity as readers and writers.

Advice for teachers of 4-year-olds

The experience of these teachers and children in the first two years of the literacy strategy indicates that it may be difficult to create a developmentally appropriate learning environment in a standard literacy hour, particularly where the needs of older children are pressing. Nevertheless, it is not impossible, and certain practices seem more likely to lead to effective teaching and learning for 4-year-olds.

- Modelling of literacy practices in shared reading and writing with whole classes can be entirely developmentally appropriate, enjoyable and effective.
- When sentence- and word-level work is focused on the needs of the youngest children it can be enjoyable and useful for them. Although the Progression in Phonics was not in use in the first year, teachers mentioned how useful this had been with all Key Stage 1 children after its introduction.

- Guided reading and writing should be used to help the youngest readers and writers to develop strategies that will help them to become independent literacy users.
- Care should be taken to avoid letting direct instruction of skills imply that creativity and exploration is bad. Children's own interpretations and attempts should be encouraged, praised and valued.
- Adults in the classroom can provide excellent opportunities to increase the youngest children's opportunities to explore and extend their understanding of reading and writing. An extra adult can give opportunities for developing the youngest children's speaking and listening skills through discussion. Teachers need to avoid letting the use of a teaching assistant inhibit children's developing independence or to lower expectations of what children can achieve independently.
- Independent activities that are no more than holding tasks to keep children busy should be avoided. Young children are more likely to learn and to keep on task with more open-ended exploratory literacy activities than overly prescribed, low-level, closed tasks.
- Developing the self-esteem of children in their early encounters with literacy in formal schooling must be a first priority if they are to flourish and make good progress.

10 Teachers and the literacy hour

Introduction

If there is to be a lasting change in the way literacy is taught, then teachers will need to change the way they think about teaching as well as the way they conduct their literacy lessons. I have already considered how some teachers seemed to be able to take the new ideas on board and incorporate them into their way of teaching whereas others changed mainly surface features such as timing. This is reflected in comments on the way in which the fluency of action in the classroom makes it difficult to change teaching style.

> Most people, like teachers, who develop expertise in a complex field of practice, rely on a repertoire of knowledge and skills which they exercise in a relatively automatic fashion much of the time. Such 'automaticity' is highly functional in a context which demands rapid and often spontaneous action, as is often the case in classrooms and schools. The 'dark side' of automaticity, however, is the thoughtless repetition of well-rehearsed solutions, even in response to problems that may require the modification of such solutions, or different solutions altogether. Cognitively demanding environments such as these are predisposed toward the exploitation of existing practices and organisational routines, and against the exploration of new routines.
>
> (Leithwood *et al.*, 1999: 15)

In addition to the views and practice of the teachers in our project, this chapter also draws on data from two questionnaires that were given to a small sample of teachers from small schools in July 1998 (*n*=104) and in July 2000 (*n*=61). In each, teachers were asked to give information about their classes and to respond to two questions that asked what they liked about the NLS and what they did not like.

Teachers' views at the outset of the NLS

During the months following the announcement of its introduction, several voices in the educational press announced their disapproval of the NLS. The major criticisms were that it:

- was rushed in its implementation,
- was based on an unevaluated pilot project,
- has an unclear rationale and lacks a theoretical basis,
- has a too tightly structured teaching hour,
- has a framework which takes away teacher autonomy,
- contains unrealistic expectations of what children can achieve,
- makes no allowances for children's cultural, economic and cognitive differences.

(See, for example, Goldstein, 1997; Haughton, 1997; Hopkins, 1997; Pyke, 1997; Sweetman, 1998.)

However, other evidence from teachers showed that, as well as their concerns, teachers did welcome various aspects of the NLS. Fisher and Lewis (1999) report that teachers responding to a questionnaire about the introduction of the literacy hour mentioned the following as aspects about which they felt positive:

- the clear structure of the framework,
- the range of new books and other materials that were being produced,
- the increased emphasis on literacy,
- the use of shared reading and writing.

A head teacher, writing in the *Times Educational Supplement* reflected the views of many teachers we met at this time:

> There are many excellent features in the literacy hour, but the time-scale is too rushed. We may well make mistakes that we would not have made if we'd had longer. Resources are a problem. Staff are feeling overloaded by having to get this going in a very short space of time. If only we could have had a year to introduce it stage by stage.
>
> (*TES*, 3 July 1998)

Responses to questionnaire, July 1998

The structure

Although comments in the press had argued that the literacy hour is too tightly structured and the Framework of Objectives takes away teacher autonomy, these were not of major concern to the teachers represented in our initial survey. Nearly 30 per cent of the teachers mentioned the structure as being one of the things they liked best. Teachers identified the 'supportive structure' and 'flexible structure' as being favourable. One Key Stage 2 teacher said, 'The National Curriculum document was far too open ended and therefore difficult to implement. This is much tighter etc. and therefore of more value.' A Key Stage 1 teacher welcomed, 'the clear, focused, hierarchical, learning objectives'.

Resources

The fact that some extra resources had been allocated to schools and that new materials were being brought out by publishers were both aspects that were welcomed by nearly 25 per cent of teachers. One Key Stage 1 class teacher commented on, 'Publishers producing superb material in big book format and money available to buy resources'. Another said, 'Lots of exciting resources – enthuses the teacher and therefore more likely to enthuse the pupils'.

Emphasis on literacy

Nearly 20 per cent of the respondents commented favourably on the greater emphasis being placed on literacy and this is reflected in their comments such as: 'That literacy is seen as important on the timetable and has a major emphasis.' And, 'The raising of standards generally. This will help in all subjects and hopefully reduce the amount of children in our schools with SEN.'

Shared text work

Nearly a quarter of teachers mentioned shared text work as being an aspect of the literacy hour about which they felt positive. This is in contrast to other sections of the hour which were only mentioned by a few teachers. Many teachers named shared reading or shared writing but gave no indication of why they felt positive about this. However, some teachers' comments implied that this type of work was already an aspect of their current practice. Two Key Stage 1 teachers' comments illustrate this, 'Shared text work and modelling as this is an approach I have always used', 'Extra time for using big books particularly for reception children to encourage a love of books.'

Other teachers mentioned the shared group experience as being motivating to children. A Key Stage 2 head teacher commented on the positive nature of 'sharing texts and learning together'.

The questionnaire analysis revealed two main areas of anxiety:

- the time required by the demands of planning for the literacy hour;
- the cost of and/or lack of resources.

Time demands

Nearly half the teachers mentioned their concern about the demands that would be made on them in the detailed planning required for the literacy hour. 'I am not happy about the increased workload, planning and the quaint notion that I and my classroom assistant (statemented child) will have lots of free time to make useful resources' wrote one early years class teacher. This reflects the views of many who wrote comments such as 'increased preparation', 'time for planning' or even, 'Time! Time!'

Resources

As reported above, several teachers felt positive about the new resources that were being introduced and the fact that some funding was being provided to assist with purchase of materials. However, resources also featured as a concern with teachers mentioning 'lack of resources', 'availability or resources', and, 'time needed to locate appropriate resources'. Five of the thirty-two teachers who mentioned a concern about resources had also listed resources as being a positive element. For example, one teacher commented favourably on the good quality resources that were being produced in preparation for the literacy hour but unfavourably on the funding needed to purchase them.

One head teacher wrote, 'Resent the whole thing! Have spent the last 2 years developing a comprehensive scheme of work for English which was commended by Ofsted. Now we get this!'

Project teachers' initial views of the hour

The twenty teachers who started the project in September 1998 had mixed views about the NLS. These can be exemplified by taking the example of three Key Stage 2 teachers who are fairly representative of the group as a whole. Nine of the twenty teachers were wholly or mainly positive about the NLS at the start of the year. Mr Ellis from Elm Primary School, who was interviewed towards the end of September, was one of these and had been implementing the literacy strategy for three weeks. In the interview he was very enthusiastic about the NLS.

> brilliant, great, smashing, wonderful, marvellous – wish we'd done it years ago . . . I must say we've got an initiative that's been properly resourced. We've got good training materials. It has been well thought out and although it's complicated I think it's going to work. If you talk to the children, I think they really like it. I think they really feel they're learning something and the reason they're learning it is I'm teaching it. I feel it sort of legitimises me to do what I'm good at which is communicating.
>
> (Interview, September 1998)

He had some reservations.

> I'd say to plan a week is taking me 2 to 3 hours at the moment. I teach phonics as the whole class lesson but I'm very aware while I'm doing that that I have children in year 6 for whom, it's not a total waste of time but it's pretty close.
>
> (Interview, September 1998)

In the start of year interview, five teachers expressed mixed feelings. Mrs Quick was one of these. She was generally positive about the forthcoming changes and was already involved in careful thinking and planning for the literacy hour. She said, 'Basically I think it is a good idea. I think the theory is extremely good. . . . I do feel it is raising [children's] literacy awareness' (interview, September 1998). This was, however, tempered with some reservations. 'I've got grave reservations about pitching it. . . . You've got to hit the highest level for those children that require that, but I do feel that half an hour of every day is definitely being lost to a number of children.' And about the shift from a more individualised approach, 'But it's that reading time, that quality time that you can give children. I don't know where you can find it, there just aren't enough hours in the day' (interview September 1998).

These reservations show concerns about differentiation issues and about the shift from a more individualised approach to the teaching of literacy. Like many of the teachers she was concerned that time to read individually with children and time for them to reflect would be lost.

Mrs Graham, on the other hand, was one of six teachers whose overall attitude showed anxiety and even hostility towards the literacy hour. She felt all the good work that was already being done had not been recognised and found the language used in the information to parents 'humiliating' for teachers. She saw the hour as being 'lots of little fragmented bits' and was concerned about children having the experience of writing at length. She found planning difficult in the literacy hour, 'You are thinking about what you need to fill in the form [planning sheet] not what the children need. You should not become unresponsive' (interview, July 1998). At the beginning of the implementation she was trying to retain spontaneity by allowing herself to follow-up children's interests and then ticking off objectives after they had been addressed.

Relationship of teachers' views to their beliefs about literacy teaching

Teachers all responded to a Teachers' Beliefs about Literacy Questionnaire (TBALQ) (Westwood *et al.*, 1987) at the beginning of the year. They had to rate themselves and respond to a series of statements designed to identify whether they favoured a structured approach to literacy teaching or a more child-centred one. There was no difference between the average score on the TBALQ of those teachers who were enthusiastic about the NLS and those who had mixed feelings. However, the average score of those who were negative about the NLS was 15 per cent higher than the other two groups, indicating that this group favoured a more child-centred approach.

Mr Ellis, who was initially most enthusiastic about the NLS, rated himself as 2 on a scale of 1 to 7, in which one indicated the most structure in teaching style, 'Directly instruct child in component skills for reading/writing'. His score of 54 out of a possible 120 put him in the 'most structured' third of the sample. Mrs Quick, who had mixed feelings, rated herself as slightly more structured than average, at 3 on the scale. Her score from the questionnaire was 61, situated in the middle of the range of teachers in the sample but her responses showed several inconsistencies in her rationale. Mrs Graham, who was negative about the NLS at first, also rated herself as slightly more structured than average, at 3 on the scale. However, her score was 66, which put her in the most 'child-centred' third of the sample with her responses lying consistently in favour of a more child-centred approach.

Relationship of their views to achievement

Despite the difference in attitudes to the literacy hour, there was no obvious relationship between initial attitude and achievement. The statistical analysis of the progress scores in reading and attitude at the start of the project revealed no significant difference. Equally, children made progress in writing in classes despite their teacher's negative attitude to the literacy hour and other children failed to make progress despite their teacher's enthusiasm for the strategy.

Teachers' views and change in practice

The relationship between teachers' attitudes to changes in their teaching and how successful or lasting any change may be is a complex one. Some writers have argued that the external imposition of change is unlikely to be successful. Hutchinson (1989) argues that top-down curriculum innovation projects are unlikely to work as they reflect a

> technological theory of change [which] will not deliver what it promises because it cannot; teachers and children may be forced to accept it at a superficial level and in so doing will be denied the opportunity of participating positively in constructing worthwhile change.
>
> (Hutchinson, 1989: 160)

However, Morris (1988) found a duality in teachers' responses to innovation. Whilst they might have a positive response to the intrinsic features of the innovation, their behaviour is determined by practical criteria such as individual ability, resources and the perceived expectations of others. This view is supported by Desforges and Cockburn (1987) in their study of mathematics teaching in the first school. They argue that teachers' frequent response to in-service courses is 'it's all very well in theory but it wouldn't work in my school'. Brown and McIntyre (1993) point out that this appears even to be the case where the innovations involve teaching strategies that are less complex than those the teachers are already using.

Unlike some initiatives, the NLS is supported by a huge infrastructure, which made it very difficult for individual teachers not to implement the strategy. Although not statutory, NLS consultants at local authority level and the national system of school inspections implied strong pressure for a national take-up of the initiative. However, for the NLS to result in something more than a change in the timing and increase in the content of literacy teaching, a wholesale change in pedagogy is required. Changing the way teachers teach is no simple endeavour as was discussed earlier, in Chapter 1.

Teachers' views at the end of the year

After a year of implementation of the NLS the project teachers were mostly somewhat happier (or less negative) about the literacy hour. Seven of the twenty teachers had become more questioning about it. Three of these could be attributed to factors within the school as much as dissatisfaction with the literacy strategy. Two others were still largely positive but had certain aspects that they were unsure about whereas their initial attitude was overwhelmingly welcoming. Two Key Stage 2 teachers, Mr Leonard and Mr Ellis, although both very enthusiastic to begin with, gradually became less and less so. After two years, both were largely negative about it and had rejected many aspects.

Teachers mentioned several factors that they felt positive about. These are listed below with the number of teachers out of the twenty who commented on each aspect indicated in brackets:

- Teachers liked working from the Framework of Objectives (11).
- Children enjoy the literacy hour (9).
- Overall children's learning had improved (9).
- They liked shared work (8).
- They enjoyed the new way of teaching (6).
- It gives increased access to a wider range of texts (6).
- It gives increased opportunities to talk about language (5).
- They felt the pace of lessons had improved (4).
- Teachers liked guided work (4).

- Children had become more independent (4).
- The NLS worked well with mixed-age classes (4).
- They found it easier to teach skills in the context of texts (2).
- It improved continuity within the school (2).
- Children's comprehension had improved (2).
- Children's spelling had improved (2).

On the other hand there were several factors that teachers referred to that they felt were not good about the literacy hour:

- There is no time for children to produce extended pieces of work (10).
- Teachers disliked the guided work (10).
- The format is inappropriate for some children (9).
- The pace of the programme of work is too pressurised (7).
- The pace within the hour is too rushed (6).
- There is too much emphasis on deconstruction of text rather than exploration at depth (6).
- It is difficult with mixed-age classes (5).
- It is too structured and repetitive (5).
- It is inappropriate for the youngest children (4).
- Teachers disliked the word-level work (3).
- Learning does not pass over into children's free writing (3).

Looking at how the three teachers described above modified their views over the year gives a better picture.

Mr Ellis

Mr Ellis, who had been very enthusiastic about the introduction of the literacy hour was still pleased with much of it and felt his class had learned a lot from it. He felt the standards of reading had improved over the year. Although our reading tests did not reflect this, a reason may be that his scores were already the highest in the pre-test. He cited the way children in his class were now much better able to analyse language and use the appropriate terminology.

> I've enjoyed the structure that it gives and I appreciate the greater control I think I've got over the curriculum because I'm planning five or six weeks in advance which I didn't always used to do I must confess. [The children] certainly know more about how language works than they did because I'm teaching it directly. I think it suits my teaching style . . . because I don't see myself as a facilitator or an enabler. I'm a teacher I think and I've always seen myself that way so it's suited the way I do things.
>
> (Interview, July 1999)

However, he also used the term 'constrained' frequently in the interview and there was a sense in which he felt less positive about using certain aspects of the hour such as guided work and word level work. Like some other teachers he also voiced concerns about aspects of English that had become neglected. He commented,

> I feel it's very important to hang on to the sort of magic of language as well. You can be too analytical, you can be too obsessed with learning objectives and you've got to hold on to what you feel is important about language and how you use it.
>
> (Interview, July 1999)

Mrs Quick

Mrs Quick had been fairly enthusiastic about the literacy hour at the start of the year but had worried about differentiation and spending enough time with individual children. Her year had been a difficult one. The school had suffered the unexpected resignation of the head teacher shortly before an Ofsted inspection and stress levels had been high. It is hardly surprising that, by the end of the year, Mrs Quick was feeling quite negative about her teaching.

She felt that children had made good progress and she had covered some things earlier than she would have in the past. However, she felt that the pace was punishing in that too much had to be covered and the short time for independent work resulted in scrappy pieces of work and that the teaching did not carry over into children's free writing.

> I think, although there's tremendous improvements in a lot of their standards of understanding, I'm not totally convinced it's coming through in the quality of the content of their work in the way that I'd like to see it. I feel that their free writing has become more inhibited despite the fact that we've planned it in. . . . You cannot sustain the pace at which the literacy hour expects you to work every week. So, although you can work in a very pacey way for a certain amount of time uh I find . . . that you cannot maintain it. It's just not sustainable in any productive form.
>
> (Interview, July 1999)

She also still had concerns about the less able children, particularly for shared text work where she found some children appeared to be left out.

Mrs Graham

Mrs Graham was still concerned about aspects of the literacy hour but this was now tempered by having decided that she liked the overall format. Her concern for the individual child showed through in that she expressed concern that not all children could keep up with the pace. Like Mrs Quick, she also found that what she had taught did not transfer into children's free writing. Although she felt it had increased the range of texts they studied she worried about the tendency to work with 'snatches' of text.

> I think we don't have the excitement of reading a book to them and us finishing it. . . . I do question all the little extracts because of the bitty way . . . the class is taught. There's all these extracts and I don't think they will go on and read any more.
>
> (Interview, July 1999)

She was particularly concerned about the relationship between planning and assessment and that it was hard to follow up on her observations of children with appropriate teaching. In her interview she would frequently mention individuals and their particular needs. She identified phonic teaching as a worry at Key Stage 2

> I'm very concerned about the phonics. . . . I feel that needs to be at this stage much more assessment-led. You're looking at what they are needing. . . . I try to pick them up from other work during the week or when I am marking something . . . particularly if I notice more than one does and try to build in that as well.
>
> (Interview, July 1999)

Teachers' views after two years

Questionnaire July 2000

Two years on from the questionnaire survey described at the beginning of this chapter, a similar questionnaire was given out at the same gathering of teachers from small schools. As before it asked two questions: one to discover what teachers felt positive about in the NLS and the second to find out what they felt negative about, or even which aspect they did not use. Sixty-one teachers responded. The themes from both questionnaires were surprisingly similar considering two years had passed. After two years, teachers were no longer concerned about the rushed introduction or enthusiastic about the emphasis on literacy. However, they were now worried about the lack of time for extended writing and the quality of work produced in the 20-minute slot, feeling this was often 'scrappy'.

The differences between the responses have been summarised in Table 10.1. Here you can see that these teachers were less concerned about the difficulty of teaching a literacy hour to mixed-age classes. There were also more opinions about the particular parts of the hour, whereas before the launch of the NLS the teachers had not been so concerned about the difficulty of particular sections.

Table 10.1   Percentage of positive and negative views about the literacy hour in 1998 and 2000

Aspect of National Literacy Strategy	1998 positive	1998 negative	2000 positive	2000 negative
Mixed-age	0	26	0	10
Structure	29	5	18	13
Resources	24	30	11	7
Raising standards	10	3	11	0
Planning	2	47	2	15
Variety of texts	6	0	20	0
Shared, text level work	23	4	56	0
Word/sentence level	13	1	16	8
Guided work	2	8	11	28
Independent work	0	6	3	5
Plenary	3	0	3	15
Time for extended writing	0	0	0	16
Poor quality work	0	0	0	16
Fun/boredom	4	7	7	8
Early years (% of KS1 teachers)	3	16	0	19

Mr Ellis

At the end of the first year, Mr Ellis had been mainly positive about the literacy hour but he used the word 'constrained' frequently in the interview. Twelve months on, he admitted he was very flexible in his use of the literacy strategy. He would use a literacy hour when he felt it suited his purposes but he would also go for weeks without using it at all. He said he did feel that his teaching of writing had improved in that it was now more focused on what children needed. But he also said he often gave children time to 'just write stories, poetry or look at words'. He expressed a concern that children could get a purely mechanistic view of language from over-emphasis on NLS objectives. He also felt that the more able pupils in his class did less well in the literacy hour because of 'all the chopping and changing'. This proved to be a revealing statement as, further questioning showed that he was trying to cover objectives for each year group in every section of the hour. It is hardly surprising that he found the hour 'mechanistic and bitty' and that the more able got 'frustrated with all the chopping and changing'. This revelation is a fascinating one. Mr Ellis is an experienced and confident head teacher. He was very positive towards the literacy hour in the beginning. He is also someone who has the confidence in his own convictions as is evidenced by his dismissal of the national assessment results for his class in favour of his own assessments – sometimes placing children higher and sometimes lower. Thus he does not seem to be the sort of person who would readily follow procedures that he found unworkable. Nevertheless he chose to abandon the literacy hour for a large part of his teaching rather than adapting it to suit his circumstances. Maybe as a teacher who favoured structure and direct teaching he felt he should be able to work in this way and persevered for this reason.

Mrs Quick

Mrs Quick is a teacher who initially had mixed feelings about the NLS. After one year in which life in her school was particularly pressurised she seemed very unhappy with the work children were doing. At the end of the second year, she was clearly much happier. She said she felt her teaching was much more focused as opposed to giving a 'woolly' introduction as before. Like other teachers she had found the NLS rather restrictive but, also like others at the end of the second year, she was beginning to reintroduce drama and role-play into her literacy teaching. She explained that she followed the Framework of Objectives rigorously but was flexible with the timing of the hour: perhaps extending the independent time to allow for drama or extended writing or omitting shared reading or writing in favour of discussion or debate about issues related to their literacy work.

She felt that what she taught did carry over into children's free writing. The school was pleased with the improved assessment results since the introduction of the NLS. She also explained that she gave children clear criteria for the expectations for each piece of writing that they did. These criteria were related closely to the NLS description of different text types. She had said at the end of the first year that she was very dissatisfied with the scrappy bits of work children produced in the literacy hour. When asked to reflect on this 12 months on, she explained that she had learned to be 'far more conscious of building a piece of work over a number of days'. Now she felt that she was able to ensure children had both the skills and the time to write a longer and more meaningful piece of written work than those they were producing in the first year.

After two years, Mrs Quick, like the others, had adapted aspects of the literacy hour to enable her to reintroduce elements of her literacy teaching that she felt she had neglected such as drama and discussion. She also had been changed in her teaching in some way by the much clearer expectations she set for writing and in her use of focused objectives. She seemed pleased that the result was improved standards in the national assessments. Her original enthusiasm for language was still reflected in her classroom but this also reflected her increased explicitness in aspects of literacy learning. Her classroom in July 2000 had several book displays on the creation and science work. She had a display of literacy information giving terms and their definitions as well as a book case with dictionaries and other reference books. She also had photos and maps on display and examples of children's written and computer work.

The lesson observed at the end of the second year reflected Mrs Quick's love of poetry and how this had rubbed off on the children.

Mrs Quick gets on well with the children in her class. She lets them know what she expects and will correct them or dole out punishments immediately if they step over boundaries. She is positive about children's work and their contributions to group discussions and will award verbal stickers and applause when responses are good. The children are responsive in the literacy hour and at times are very keen to answer. Mrs Quick's love of poetry has obviously rubbed off on the class, as they spontaneously will recite chunks of poems.

(Field notes, July 2000)

However, although she emphasised how much more structured and focused her teaching had become with her use of the framework of objectives the observer notes

The lesson today reflected . . . teacher-composed objectives. However, it wasn't clear in the lesson what she was getting at. She used closed questions a lot to get children to come up with bits of information and they did compare poems but teacher didn't really explain why they were doing that i.e. purpose or the usefulness.

(Field notes, July 2000)

Although there is insufficient evidence to draw any conclusions here, there is a sense in which this teacher's improvement in her teaching as she sees it may be more in her own mind than in reality.

Mrs Graham

Mrs Graham had been very negative about the literacy hour in the begin-ning in that she felt it inhibited her ability to match work to the needs of individuals. Although after a year she found she liked the format, she still had concerns about individual children. Two years on, she was much more positive. She said she felt her teaching had become much more methodical. Interestingly, she said she no longer worried about children not getting something the first time as she realised it will come up again. She said she felt under less pressure to have to cover it all at once. She was still concerned that too much focus on the technical aspects of the NLS made it difficult for children to put it all together to develop a coherent under-standing of the whole. She did also say that she was getting better at linking work in the literacy hour with work in other subjects and in this way she felt she was able to counter-balance the potentially decon-textualised work in the literacy hour.

In July 2000, her classroom was a lively environment with displays reflecting work on the topic on the village. There were posters, labelled diagrams, photographs with accompanying questions, a time line, maps as well as examples of children's writing of poems, descriptions and so on. It seemed that Mrs Graham has been able to take on the NLS, albeit reluctantly, and develop her own teaching style within it. After two years she seemed to be happier with her literacy teaching. Like Mrs Quick, she had reintroduced aspects of her teaching that had been omitted in the first year of the NLS. Also like Mrs Quick, she felt she had become more focused in her teaching. However, the observer's field notes again question this:

> Mrs Graham appears to have a good positive relationship with the children. She encourages them to articulate their thoughts and develop opinions and take responsibility for their work. The children respond enthusiastically. . . . Today connectives were the focus and they had been addressed in a previous lesson . . . that may be why Mrs Graham did not introduce them fully. However, she never explains what connectives do in a sentence or gives examples of how they are used. The closest she gets to a definition is that they 'make your writing flow' and they 'help you with your writing'. She puts up a list of connectives for children to draw on in their own writing and a few extras on a flip chart, e.g. nonetheless, whenever. She asks the children what they notice about these, prompting for they are made up of small words and eventually gets this answer. However another child answers that all except 'although' begin with consonants . . . this seems so off the point.
>
> (Field notes, July 2000)

Change to teaching – real or imagined?

An example from a literacy hour observed after two years of implementation gives a further indication that some teachers, although teaching a literacy hour in terms of the time division of the lesson, have still not changed their practice in any fundamental way. The approach to the teaching of literacy in the 1980s and 1990s often involved the teacher providing a stimulus about which children would then talk, or read, or write while the teacher would draw out any teaching opportunities that would occur. The NLS, on the other hand, expects teachers to select one or two pre-specified objectives that will be taught using a text that has been chosen for its suitability for the purpose. In the lesson observed here, Mrs Freeman was addressing a text level objective 'to discuss meanings of words and phrases that create humour, and sound effects in poetry, e.g. nonsense poems, tongue twisters . . .' (DfEE, 1998 year two, term three, text eight). The lesson started with her showing a large picture of a sandwich, she discussed with children what was in the sandwich in the picture and what sort of sandwiches they enjoyed. In this she was perfectly justifiably linking the 'text' with children's own experiences. Children joined in enthusiastically sharing their likes and dislikes of sandwiches. When she then introduced a tongue twister about a sandwich, they were engaged and interested in the contents of the sandwich rather than the words the poet used to gain effect. The observer wrote,

> however, what actually happened was they heard several tongue twisters, joined in a bit and talked about the definition of a tongue twister. The teacher announced they were doing tongue twisters today but she didn't say what they were doing with them or why they were doing them or what they were meant to be learning from the lesson.
>
> (Field notes, June 2000)

Mrs Freeman felt her teaching had improved over the two years in that it was now more structured and focused. She said that she now felt happy that what she was doing within the strategy was better matched to her class. However, it is clear from the example given above that although her planning is focused and related to the Framework of Objectives, the way it is taught may be very similar to what she was doing before.

Summary

Thus it seems we have a group of teachers most of whom who have adopted the NLS into their teaching. Maybe, views have moderated from wildly enthusiastic to cautious or from openly hostile to cautiously positive. Teachers certainly feel planning from the Framework of Objectives has tightened up their teaching. Most seem to regret losing some of the freedom they enjoyed before but many are managing to reintroduce those more creative parts of their teaching into the literacy hour. They seem to have the confidence to adapt and develop the framework to fit their perceived needs. Although the sample here is too small to draw conclusions, there is some evidence that changes in teachers' teaching style may be more in their own minds than in actual fact. It would be unfair and untrue to say that there had been no fundamental change to teaching over the two years of the project. However, there are indications that some of the teachers' increased confidence with the literacy hour arises from the way they have adapted the NLS to their teaching, as much as adapting their teaching to the NLS.

11 Implications for research, policy and practice

Introduction

This research has covered the first two years of the implementation of the NLS in primary schools throughout England. Described as 'the most ambitious attempt ever in this country to change for the better teaching approaches across the entire education service' (DfEE, 1997: para. 27), the NLS has undoubtedly had a huge impact on how teachers teach reading and writing. I have tried to show here what happened in individual classrooms and to draw out what may have contributed to success in teaching and what may have been less helpful. Our research certainly revealed changes in the ways teachers planned and conducted their teaching but it also points to some of the changes being less marked than teachers themselves thought. I have tried to show that teaching is a complex process and one that is not easily altered. There are too many factors other than the purely technical features that contribute to a successful classroom. The teachers' own views about literacy and literacy learning; the quality of the interaction that takes place within the classroom; the age, experience, maturity, learning style of the learner all contribute to the context within which the learning takes place.

Teaching in the literacy hour

Increased direct teaching

The NLS was introduced with the intention of increasing the amount of direct teaching that teachers use in their literacy teaching and to maximise the impact of this. This has involved increasing considerably the amount of whole class and group teaching and reducing the time teachers spend with individuals. From the evidence of the schools in our project, this has certainly happened. Teachers readily took on shared reading and increasingly used shared writing. The range of aspects of literacy that is taught seems to have increased. Our teachers spoke of increased time and extended content of their phonics teaching at Key Stage 1 and of grammar teaching at Key Stage 2. They found guided group work harder to implement, although many teachers worked around this by reading or writing with groups during free or extended reading and writing periods at other times in the day or week. Some teachers have found the plenary difficult, though this seems mainly to have been because they have misunderstood its function as a way of reinforcing objectives. Certainly there is less time for teachers to spend reading, writing or talking with individual children.

Contrary to the expectations of some teachers, children enjoy the literacy hour. They have found the increased range of texts interesting and enjoyed the big books. The game-like approach to phonics proposed by Progression in Phonics (DfEE, 1999) has been well received, as have some of the investigative techniques used in grammar and vocabulary work. Also, contrary to expectations, less able children seem to have benefited from the experience of 'reading' more challenging texts and being included in whole class parts of the literacy hour.

The NLS Framework of Objectives claims that the most successful teaching has a clear focus and direction, and is discursive, interactive, well-paced, confident and ambitious (DfEE, 1998: 8). I have tried to show what this meant in these classrooms. There are questions about the extent to which all teachers were able to implement this style of teaching, and, when they did, whether there were still important elements of successful teaching that were missing.

Teaching with clear focus and direction

Nearly all the teachers after one and two years of the NLS said they felt their teaching had become more structured and focused. Certainly, their planning contained more specific objectives and covered a wider range of aspects of literacy. However, I have tried to show that the way these teachers went about teaching in the literacy hour varied. Either some teachers' enthusiasm for the text or their concern to involve all children made them cover a whole range of ideas and thoughts. Although they felt their teaching was focused, this focus was not always clear to the observer or, maybe, the children. Other teachers tended to take the product as the focus of the lesson as opposed to the learning; for example the production of a particular type of text rather than examining how different forms of language affect the meaning or the impact of a text.

Discursive and interactive teaching

The NLS describes their model of teaching as 'discursive – characterised by high quality oral work'; and 'interactive – pupils' contributions are encouraged, expected and extended' (DfEE, 1998: 8). Others have pointed to the difficulty of achieving high-quality interaction in whole class situations (Moyles *et al.*, 2000; Mroz *et al.*, 2000). The teachers in this study used questioning effectively to engage different children in the whole class sessions. They used questions to differentiate, to monitor understanding and to ensure involvement. However, only a few teachers used questions to challenge and extend children's thinking. The necessity of keeping a good pace and clear focus resulted in the interaction being essentially controlling. The teacher led and children followed. In many classes this worked successfully and children seemed involved and enthusiastic about this literacy work. Nevertheless, it must be recognised that this may have been to the detriment of creative or divergent thinking. It may be that in this type of classroom atmosphere literacy is increasingly seen as an artefact of the teacher with a resulting loss of relevance for those very children that the literacy hour is intended to help.

Well-paced teaching

The NLS claims that successful teaching is well-paced, 'there is a sense of urgency, driven by the need to make progress and succeed' (DfEE, 1998: 8). Teachers' interpretations of this varied. There were those teachers who were worried by the number and challenge of the teaching objectives for each term and there were those teachers who found the timing of the literacy hour restrictive. Some teachers felt pressurised in their teaching and maintained that this pressure did not lead to quality learning. They talked of 'bittiness' and being on a 'whistle stop tour'. These impressions receded in the second year as teachers gained confidence in adapting the framework and the hour to suit the perceived needs of their own classes. It seems that 'with a sense of purpose' would be a better description than 'well-paced' as it removes the connotations of time and highlights reasoned activity as opposed to activity for activity's sake.

Confident teaching

This is seen as teaching in which teachers have a clear understanding of the objectives. The teachers who took part in this project almost uniformly said that they felt their knowledge of literacy had increased through their teaching of the NLS. We certainly judged that those teachers who had a good grounding in English subject knowledge were better able to teach the objectives in a way that seemed likely to make sense to children. This was particularly the case in teaching knowledge about language where rules or peripheral facts were taught as opposed to the purpose or use of the feature of language. For example, teaching that connectives are often made up of two or more little words (e.g. nevertheless, however), rather than teaching what connectives are used for and how they affect meaning shows a lack of real understanding of language.

Ambitious teaching

Teachers are expected to have 'optimism about and high expectations of success' (DfEE, 1998: 8). Without doubt, many of our teachers expressed surprise in the interviews at the end of the first and second years of the NLS at how well their children had managed and how much they had enjoyed the challenge. Yet it became clear that just having challenging objectives was not enough to ensure ambitious teaching. Some teachers felt that the NLS had too high expectations of young children's ability to work independently. These teachers invariably had children who were slow to develop independence, aptly illustrating the impact of the teachers' expectations. Other teachers worked carefully to provide for and develop independent working strategies. These teachers had much more success. This was connected to teachers' expectations about what literacy activities children could be expected to do inside and outside the hour. Teachers whose expectations were low were more likely to set closed or mechanical tasks. This may have involved a teaching assistant helping the youngest children copy a sentence or asking year 6 children to fill in the blanks on a writing frame to produce writing to fit a particular formula. Teachers with higher expectations would be more likely to ask the teaching assistant to help 4-year-olds develop role play around a key text or to encourage year 6 children to compose a parody on a particular text genre.

What was missing in the literacy hour

The first year of implementation showed the teachers on this project working hard to follow the Framework of Objectives and the guidance for the literacy hour. Initially there was concern about the amount of time that was being taken up for literacy and numeracy teaching. Two aspects that gave particular cause for concern were the apparently low status afforded to oral language and the loss of an emphasis on language across the curriculum. As the year progressed concern also grew about the lack of time for children to reflect on their learning or to pursue anything to any depth. It is not really possible to comment in detail upon these important issues as our research only collected evidence of what happened in the literacy hour. Any idea of what went on at other times only came from observing evidence around the classroom such as displays and from what teachers told us.

Speaking and listening

The importance of speaking and listening in the curriculum cannot be understated. Oral language is of great importance both as a skill in itself because of the role it plays in learning. The introduction of a literacy strategy seemed to downplay the importance of oral language. As discussed above, there is concern that the style of interaction implied by the NLS discourages exploratory talk. Increased whole class teaching reduces the amount of time teachers can spend interacting with individuals. However, in all whole class sessions children were encouraged to contribute in some way or another – more so maybe than they might have been in the kind of introductory whole class session that teachers said they used before the literacy hour. Indeed, one Key Stage 2 pupil when asked if he liked the literacy hour replied, 'It's great, you get to talk more.' At the end of the second year of the NLS most of the twelve teachers we revisited referred to a whole range of things that went on in their classrooms to develop children's speaking and listening: circle time, sharing news, drama, talking about books. Without doubt, there is no place for complacency. Oral language has long been the neglected part of the English curriculum and we should not let ourselves be influenced so much by working to national assessments that we neglect other important areas.

Language across the curriculum

At the outset of the NLS some teachers welcomed the increased focus on literacy teaching while others regretted the loss of opportunities to develop language and literacy in other curricular contexts. Here again, teachers worked hard to deliver the objectives in the literacy hour in the first year. By the second year as their confidence with the framework grew, they were better able to relate what they were doing in literacy with other curriculum areas and to use work in other curriculum areas to contextualise the literacy objectives. Arguably, teachers' increased understanding of language that they have gained from the NLS can only help them develop literacy throughout the curriculum.

Time for reflection

Without doubt well-paced, focused, direct teaching does not appear to value reflection. Many would say that there is little time in today's world to reflect and that classrooms imitate this with the relentless striving to meet targets and raise standards. Some of these teachers raised concerns about the lack of time for children to reflect on their learning or for consolidation. As they gained confidence with the NLS they began to develop ways of remedying this:

- They introduced time outside the literacy hour when children could read together or talk about books.
- Teachers of the youngest children began to think again about opportunities for play.
- Other teachers reintroduced drama, sharing time and other less goal-oriented classroom activities.
- Within the literacy hour, teachers gave brief opportunities for children to talk in pairs or try out bits of composition before moving on. Whilst these are too short for reflection they do provide ways for children to try out their own ideas rather than merely giving the teacher the 'right' answer.

- A few teachers thought about planning collaborative group work in independent time – particularly oral work that had no fixed product.

The needs of the individual within the whole class

Also in the second year of the NLS, teachers began to incorporate setting of individual learning targets. Whereas in the first year, teachers were very concerned to plan and teach to the objectives, as their understanding of the Framework grew they felt better able to adapt the NLS to cater for their particular class. This was of mixed benefit. For some teachers it enabled them to retain the focus and increased coverage of the literacy curriculum at the same time as using the Framework flexibly to address the needs of individuals and groups within the class. For other teachers this was more problematic as it enabled them to reintroduce or revert to familiar practice, which had not been effective in the past.

Advice for teachers

It is, I am sure, no surprise to anyone that the results of this research point to there being no simple solution to the problem of how best to ensure that all children receive the best literacy teaching possible. The NLS has influenced the way teachers plan and teach but there is still considerable variation in how successful this is. To a large extent, success depends on the confidence and talent of the individual teacher. No formula can create an effective teacher. Whilst teachers can be informed by research into effective teaching, they also need to take into account what we know about how children develop and learn. Teaching is a complex interaction between the subject, the learner, the teacher and the social context. Whereas in the past we may have been guilty of placing too much emphasis on the learner, we must not fall into the trap of being beguiled by an oversimplistic model of direct instruction. The picture of teaching in the literacy hour presented here points to certain important points:

- Focused, direct teaching is effective when it is supported by knowledge of the subject and the child.
- High-quality, pacey interaction can be fun and helpful in developing understanding but it can become no more than a quiz show if there is no time for reflection and exploration of ideas.
- Tasks children are given to do to practice and extend their understanding can be either limiting or challenging depending on the extent to which they allow the child to explore the process of literacy rather than just produce a preordained product.
- Oral language is essential to effective learning. Nearly all children can talk in pairs and small groups. Making use of this fact gives opportunities for worthwhile independent activities that can be challenging without being limited to the most able.

- Literacy and language learning is relevant across the whole curriculum. There is no reason why planning in the school for literacy cannot take into account what is going on in other subjects. Topic work will no longer lead the curriculum but sharing topics in two or more subjects can help show the relevance and purpose of what is bring learned.
- The Framework of Objectives should be looked on as a flexible support not a straightjacket. Grouping objectives, reordering text types, revisiting previously covered objectives can be effective ways of catering for the needs of particular children within specific contexts.
- The model of teaching presented by the NLS which moves from scaffolded to independent learning, in which the teacher demonstrates and models how readers and writers think and act, which maximises the potential of the teacher's time without losing sight of the individual is what is important.

Advice for policy-makers

The international team of evaluators from Ontario remind policy-makers of 'the power of professional learning communities' and that 'dissenting voices contribute to clear thinking' (Earl *et al.*, 2000: 40–1). One of the biggest concerns these teachers had was the sense of powerlessness that certain aspects of the NLS made them feel. If teachers are to continue to develop as effective teachers of literacy they need to feel that their views are listened to and valued. They can learn from each other as well as from those whose job it is to inform and instruct them in the ways of the NLS. There is a danger that the model of in-service and dissemination of NLS materials will perpetuate the controlling, directive view of the NLS into a style of classroom teaching that could limit and alienate some learners. Evidence from this research seems to point to teachers doing their best to teach the way the NLS has asked them to. However, how this develops depends on the capacity of the individual to understand the pedagogy as well as learn the strategies. Direct instruction without time and space to reflect and explore ideas does not make effective teachers nor effective literacy users.

Indications for further research

This research has done no more than provide a snapshot of a handful of classes in the first two years of the NLS. However, it supports some of the criticisms levelled against the strategy but also shows that it has influenced, often in a positive way, the teaching of literacy. There are particular areas that clearly need further research if we are to continue to influence policy-makers in the way literacy teaching moves in the years to come. In particular:

- The nature and impact of interaction in the classroom in whole class and small group contexts.
- Identification of strategies that facilitate reflection and exploration of literacy.
- Ways of engaging teachers in the pedagogy of literacy as well as the content.
- Further exploration of the teaching of writing, how this develops and the most effective ways of facilitating this.

Appendices

Appendix I: interview schedules at the start and end of the year

Interview 1 1998

Semi-structured interview   Date:_____

School number:_____   Teacher code:_____

Begin by reminding the teacher of confidentiality, these answers only to be used for research purposes, etc.

How long have you been teaching in a small school?

Current practice – teaching style
Moving on to focus upon teaching, how do you currently organise and plan for your class to allow for different age groups? *Prompt for*

- Flexibility
- Differentiation
- Use of whole class teaching and how long been doing this

Current practice – English
Moving to the teaching of the English How do you currently plan for English? Do not forget to collect sample of 1998 long-, medium- and short-term planning (pre-NLS)

What particular targets has your school identified in literacy?

How do you currently teach reading? *Prompt for*

- Scheme/non-scheme/other reading material
- Hearing children read, individual, group, shared reading
- The role of phonics
- Sight vocabulary
- Books going home
- Parental involvement
- Other adults in the classroom

What are your current resources for reading?

How do you currently teach writing? *Prompt for views on / use of*

- developmental approach (emergent writing)
- modelled writing (teacher leading composition)
- shared writing (teacher scribe, children composing)
- process? How often? (plan, draft, edit etc.)
- range of types of writing – fiction/non-fiction etc.
- emphasis placed on grammar and punctuation?
       How taught ?

NB probe for conceptual understanding of why they do these things.

If they have not already answered these questions, ask:

What are your current resources for writing?
How do you currently teach handwriting ?
What are your resources for handwriting?
How do you currently teach spelling?
What are your resources for spelling?

Then:

How do you currently assess in English? *Prompt for*

- formal/ informal
- reading writing /speaking and listening

How did you spend your £1000?

If they have not yet spent it do they have any thoughts about how they plan to spend it?

Have you changed your practice at all in the last two years ? If so, how and why?

Literacy hour

Moving on to the literacy hour
What are your current feelings about the literacy hour?
What is your current state of planning for the literacy hour ?
How do you predict it will impact upon you? Your pupils?
What changes do you anticipate making in your classroom from September?
What aspects of this initiative do you see as being helpful to you and your pupils?
What aspects of this initiative do you see as being problematic for you and your pupils?
Before we end, is there anything you would like to say about the literacy hour and/or your teaching of English?

Interview 2 1999

Semi-structured interview 2   Date:_____

School number:_____   **Teacher code:**_____

Begin by reminding the teacher of confidentiality, these answers only to be used for research purposes, etc.

Now that we're a year into the NLS, how do you feel about the literacy hour?

Change

Has your teaching changed over the year? *Prompt for*

• Pace
• Style
• Content
• Organisation

Can you tell me what the positive and negative aspects of the literacy hour are?

• Let's start with the positive ... now what are you less positive about?

Do you plan to do things differently next year?

Mixed ages

How are you finding the literacy hour works with mixed-age classes?
How have you used the Framework of Objectives for mixed-age classes?
How else have you differentiated for mixed-age classes?

Format

Is there any aspect of the literacy hour that you don't use regularly?
How much do you keep to your planned objectives?

Independence

One of the concerns at the beginning of the year was what would happen in independent group time and whether the children would work independently, productively.

• How are you finding this?
• How did you achieve this?

- Examples of classroom management techniques, nature of tasks, scaffolding.

Has independence progressed or increased over the year?
If you had one thing that would be helpful to other teachers of mixed-age classes, what would that be?

Appendix II: observation schedule for literacy hour

Observation schedule for literacy hours

TEACHER CODE:

VISIT NUMBER:

DATE:

TIME:

LAYOUT VARIATION:

LITERACY HOUR CONTEXT

Notes:

OBSERVATION NUMBER

OBSERVER LOCATION:

WHOLE CLASS T S/W   OTHER   ALLOCATING WORK   GUIDED   INDEPENDENT   PLENARY   CHANGEOVER

NUMBER OF PUPILS

LOCATION
Seated   on floor   at tables
Standing

TEACHER   Seated   Standing

RESOURCES

Time   Teacher activity

Appendix III: observation schedule for target children

Observation schedule for target children

Whole class 15 mins	Whole class 15 mins	Independent/Guided	Plenary	Notes

Appendix IV: questionnaire and interview schedule at end of the second year

Follow-up questionnaire June/July 2000

The implementation of the literacy hour in small rural schools

An ESRC-funded research project, University of Plymouth

How many times do you usually teach a literacy hour each week?

In your literacy hours, how many times do you do the following in a week, on average:

- Shared reading
- Shared writing
- Word level work
- Sentence level
- Guided reading
- Guided writing
- Plenary

On a day when you do not do a literacy hour, what language work do you do?

On days when you do have a literacy hour, what other language work do you do?

Do you use specific objectives the NLS Framework of Objectives?

	Yes	*No*
For all your language work		
For every literacy hour		
For most literacy hours		
For less than half the literacy hours		
Rarely		
Never		

When you do not use the NLS Framework of Objectives, how do you choose your teaching focus?

Which aspects of the literacy hour do you like best?

Which do you like least?

What have been the major changes in your literacy teaching in the last two years?

Follow-up interview June/July 2000

What do you think has improved in your teaching reading or writing since pre-NLS?

What, if anything, do you think has been lost in your teaching of reading and writing since pre-NLS?

Do you feel that what you teach is showing up in children's free writing?

How many of the training materials (lunch box) have you used?

How did you use them? As suggested or individually?

Appendix V: ethics protocol

Statement of ethical principles

Ethical considerations

All research undertaken by staff of the University of Plymouth must conform to the University's Research Ethics Code of Conduct. This research will conform fully to the Code of Conduct.

Openness, honesty and informed consent

The permission of head teachers and participating class teachers will be sought prior to the start of the project and the aims and methodology of the proposed research will be fully explained. A written résumé of the research rationale and a timetable of the data collection will be sent to each participating school. As no children will be identified as individuals, the consent of children to take part will not be sought. However, at the start of the project the children will be given a simple explanation (appropriate to their age), of the nature and purposes of the research. There are no apparent risks attached to becoming involved in the research study but the research team will be alert for any potential risks should they arise, and will take steps to protect the participants and researchers from physical or psychological harm.

Right to withdraw

Schools will be informed in writing that they have the right to withdraw at any stage of the study.

Confidentiality and anonymity

The schools and individual participants will be informed of their right to confidentiality. Pseudonyms for individuals and schools will be used in any documents that arise from the study. Data will be kept securely and any records of participants' names will be kept separate from the data.

Impartiality

Each member of the research team will endeavour to be impartial in their approach to the research, the data collection, the analysis and reporting of the results. All data will be recorded and will be open to external scrutiny. Peer examination will be invited during the project.

References

Adams, M. J. (1990) *Beginning to Read: Thinking and Learning about Print*, Cambridge, Massachusetts: MIT Press.

Ahlberg, J. and Ahlberg, A. (1986) *The Jolly Postman: or Other People's Letters*, London: Heinemann.

Alexander, R. (1988) 'Garden or Jungle? Teacher development and informal primary education' in A. Blyth (ed.) *Informal Primary Education Today*, Lewis, East Sussex: Falmer Press.

Alexander, R. (1992) *Policy and Practice in Primary Education*, London: Routledge.

Alexander, R., Rose, A. J. and Woodhead, C. (1992) *Curriculum Organisation and Classroom Practice in Primary Schools: a Discussion Paper*, London: Department of Education.

Alexander, R., Wilcocks, J. and Nelson, N. (1995) 'Discourse, Pedagogy and the National Curriculum: change and continuity in primary schools', *Research Papers in Education* 11(1): 81–120.

Anderson, J. (1995) 'How parents perceptions of literacy learning relate to their children's emerging literacy knowledge', *Reading Horizons* 35(3): 207–28.

Ashworth, J. and Clark, J. (1993) *Where's my Baby?* London: Nelson Paperback.

Ausubel, D. P. (1968) *Educational Psychology: A Cognitive View*, New York: Holt, Rineheart and Winston.

Barrett, G. (1989) *Disaffection for School? The Early Years*, London: Falmer Press.

Beard, R. (1999) *National Literacy Strategy: Review of Research and Other Related Evidence*, London: Department for Education and Employment.

Beard, R. (2002) 'As the research predicted? Examining the success of the National Literacy Strategy', in R. Fisher, G. Brooks and M. Lewis (eds) *Raising Standards of Literacy*, London: Falmer Press.

Bennett, N., Desforges, C., Cockburn, A. and Wilkinson, B. (1984) *The Quality of Pupil Learning Experiences*, London: Lawrence Erlbaum Associates.

Bell, A. and Sigsworth, A. (1987) *The Small Rural Primary School*, London, Falmer Press.

Beverton, S and English, E. (1999) Paper given at UKRA Conference, Chester.

Bickler, S. (1999) 'Creating a Mental Set for Learning', in R. Fisher with H. Arnold, (eds) *Understanding the Literacy Hour*, Royston: United Kingdom Reading Association.

Borich, G. (1986) *Effective Teaching Methods* 3rd edn, New York: Macmillan.

Brooks, G. (1998) 'Trends in literacy standards 1948–1996', *Language and Literacy News*, Spring: 3–4.

Brophy, J. (1986) 'Teaching and learning mathematics: where research should be going', *Journal for Research in Mathematics Education* 17: 323–46.

Brophy, J. E. and Good, T. L. (1986) 'Teacher behaviour and student achievement', in M. C. Whittrock (ed.) *Handbook of Research on Teaching*, New York: Macmillan.

Brown, S. and McIntyre, D. (1993) *Making Sense of Teaching*, Buckingham: Open University Press.

Browne, A. (1991) *Willy and Hugh*, London: Julia MacRae.

Bruner, J. (1977) 'Early social interaction and language development', in H. R. Schaffer (ed.) *Studies in Mother Child Interaction*, London: Academic Press.

Bruner, J. (1983) *Child's Talk: Learning to Use Language*, Oxford: Oxford University Press.

Bruner, J. and Haste, H. (1987) *Making Sense, The Child's Construction of the World*, London: Methuen.

Cambourne, B. (1999) 'Conditions for learning: explicit and systematic teaching of reading – a new slogan?' *The Reading Teacher* 52(2): 126–7.

Chall, J. S. (1967) *Learning to Read; the Great Debate*, New York: McGraw-Hill.

Clark, J. (1991) *Along Came Eric*, London: Anderson Press.

Clark, C. M. and Peterson, P. L. (1986) 'Teachers' thought processes', in M. C. Whittrock (ed.) *Handbook of Research on Teaching*, 3rd edn, New York: Macmillan.

Cook-Gumperz, J. (1986) *The Social Construction of Literacy*, Cambridge: Cambridge University Press.

Dadds, M. (1999) 'Teachers' values and the literacy hour', in *Cambridge Journal of Education* 29(1): 7–19.

Department for Education and Employment (1997) *The Implementation of the National Literacy Strategy*, London: Department for Education and Employment.

Department for Education and Employment (1998) *The National Literacy Strategy: Framework for Teaching*, London: Department for Education and Employment.

Department for Education and Employment (1999) *Progression in Phonics*, London: Department for Education and Employment.

Department for Education and Employment (2000a) *2000 National Test Results* Online. Available HTTP: http/www.dfee.gov.uk 20 September 2000.

Department for Education and Employment (2000b) *The National Literacy Strategy Guidance on the Organisation of the National Literacy Strategy in Reception classrooms* DfEE 0153/2000, 09/00, London: Department for Education and Employment.

Department of Education and Science (1967) *Children and their Primary Schools*, London: HMSO.

Department of Education and Science (1978) *Primary Education in England*, London: HMSO.

Department of Education and Science (1982) *Education 5–9: an Illustrative Survey of 80 First Schools in England*, London: HMSO.

Department of Education and Science (1988) *English for Ages 5–11* (The Cox Report), London: HMSO.

Department of Education and Science (1990) *Starting with Quality*, report of the Committee of Enquiry into the quality of the educational experience offered 3 and 4 year olds, chaired by Angela Rumbold. London: DES.

Department of Education, Employment, Training: Victoria (1997) *Teaching Readers in the Classroom Early Years Literacy Program Stage 1*, South Melbourne, Victoria: Addison Wesley Longman.

Department of Education, Employment, Training: Victoria (1998) *Teaching Writers in the Classroom Early Years Literacy Program Stage 2*, South Melbourne, Victoria: Addison Wesley Longman.

Department of Education, Employment, Training: Victoria (1999) *Teaching Speakers and Listeners in the Classroom Early Years Literacy Program Stage 3*, South Melbourne, Victoria: Addison Wesley Longman.

Desforges, C. and Cockburn, A. (1987) *Understanding the Mathematics Teacher*, Lewis, East Sussex: Falmer Press.

Devon Curriculum Services (1998) *Literacy Hour in Small Schools*, Exeter: Devon Curriculum Services.

Donaldson, M. (1978) *Children's Minds*, London: Fontana Books.

Earl. L., Fullan, M., Leithwood, K. and Watson, N. (2000*) Watching and Learning: First Annual Report of OISE/UT Evaluation of the Implementation of the National Literacy and Numeracy Strategies*, Toronto: Ontario Institute for Studies in Education, University of Toronto.

Edwards, D. and Mercer, N. (1987) *Common Knowledge: The Development of Understanding in the Classroom*, London: Methuen.

Farjeon, E. (1996) *Cats Sleep Anywhere*, London: Frances Lincoln.

Fisher, Robert (1995) *Teaching Children to Learn*, Cheltenham: Stanley Thornes.

Fisher, R. (2000) 'Developmentally appropriate practice and a national literacy strategy', *British Journal of Educational Studies* 48(1): 58–69.

Fisher, R. and Lewis, M. (1999) 'Anticipation or trepidation; teachers' views on the introduction of the literacy hour', *Reading* 33(1): 29–35.

Fullan, M. (1999) *The Return of Large-Scale Reform*, Toronto: Ontario Institute for Studies in Education, University of Toronto.

Galton, M. and Patrick, H. (1990) *Curriculum Provision in the Small Primary School*, London: Routledge.

Galton, M., Simon, B. and Croll, P. (1980) *Inside the Primary Classroom*, London: Routledge.

Galton, M., Hargreaves, L., Comber, C., Wall, D. and Pell, A. (1999) *Inside the Primary Classroom: 20 Years on*, London: Routledge.

Garner, R. (1980) 'Monitoring of understanding: an investigation of good and poor readers' awareness of induced miscomprehension of text', *Journal of Reading Behaviour* 12: 55–63.

Geekie, P., Cambourne, B. and Fitzsimmons, P. (1999) *Understanding Literacy Development*, Stoke on Trent: Trentham Books.

Gipps, C. (1992) *What We Know about Effective Teaching*, London: University of London, Institute of Education.

Goldstein H, (1997) 'Labour Party Literacy Task Force Report: a critique', *Education-line*. Available at www.leeds.ac.uk/educol

Goodacre, E. (1971) *Children and Learning to Read*, London: Routledge

Gorman, T. and Fernandez, C (1992) *Reading in Recession: a Report of the Comparative Reading Survey from the Centre for Research in Language and Communication*, Slough: NFER.

Gray, N. and Wilcox, C. (1994) *Sharron and Darren*, London: Young Lions.

Hall, L. (1987) 'Come back teacher', *Times Educational Supplement*, 16 October, p. 24.

Harber, C. (1996) *Small Schools and Democratic Practice,* Nottingham: Educational Heretics Press.

Haughton, E (1997) 'One Hour to change the world', in Extras and Update section *Times Educational Supplement,* 27 June.

Heath, S. B. (1983) *Ways with Words: Language, Life and Work in Communities and Classrooms,* New York: Cambridge University Press.

Hoffman, (1998) 'When bad things happen to good ideas in literacy education: professional dilemmas, personal decisions, and political traps', *The Reading Teacher* 52(2): 102–13.

Holdaway, D. (1979) *The Foundations of Literacy,* Sydney: Aston Scholastic.

Hopkins, D. (1997) 'Dangers of imposing an untested policy', in Extras and Update. *Times Educational Supplement* 12 September.

Hopkins, D. and Ellis, P. D. (1991) 'The effective small primary school: some significant factors', *School Organisation* 11(1): 115–22.

Hurst, V. 1997 *Planning for Early Learning,* 2nd edn, London: Paul Chapman Publishing.

Hutchinson, B. (1989) 'Teachers' models of change and proposals for educational reform', *Cambridge Journal of Education* 19(2): 153–62.

Katz, L. G., Evangelou, D. and Hartman, J.A. (1990) *The Case for Mixed-age Grouping in Early Education* Washington, DC: National Association for the Education of Young Children.

King Smith, D. (1990) *The Jolly Witch,* London: Simon and Schuster.

Langer, E. (1997) *The Power of Mindful Learning,* New York: Addison-Wesley.

Leithwood, K., Jantzi, D. and Mascall, B. (1999) *Large-scale Reform: What Works?,* Toronto: Ontario Institute for Studies in Education, University of Toronto.

Mason, J. (1992) 'Reading stories to pre-literate children: a proposed connection to reading', in P. Gough, L. Ehri and R. Treiman (eds) *Reading Acquisition,* Hillsdale, NJ: Lawrence Erlbaum Associates.

Medwell, J., Wray, D., Poulson, L. and Fox, R. (1998) *Effective Teachers of Literacy: a Report of a Research Project Commissioned by the Teacher Training Agency,* Exeter: University of Exeter.

Ministry of Education (1994) *English National Curriculum,* Wellington, New Zealand: Ministry of Education.

Morris, P. (1988) Teachers' attitudes towards a curriculum innovation: an East Asian study', *Research in Education* 40: 75–85.

Mortimore, P., Sammons, P., Stoll, L. and Ecob, R. (1988) *School Matters: The Junior Years,* London: Open Books.

Moyles, J., Merry, R., Hislam, J., Hunter-Carsch, M., Kitson, J., Paterson, A.S.F., Hargreaves, L., English, E and Sarries, V. (2000) 'Ready steady sprint! interactive teaching in the primary school', paper given at British Educational Research Association Conference, Cardiff.

Mroz, M., Smith, F. and Hardman, F. (2000) 'The discourse of the literacy hour', *Cambridge Journal of Education* 30(3): 379–90.

Office of National Statistics (1996) *General Household Survey for 1995,* London: The Stationery Office.

Office for Standards in Education (1993) *Boys and English,* London: Ofsted.

Office for Standards in Education (1995) *English: A Review of Inspection Findings 1993/4,* London: Ofsted.

Office for Standards in Education (1996) *The Teaching of Reading in 45 Inner*

London Primary Schools: A report by Her Majesty's Inspectors in Collaboration with the LEAs of Islington, Southwark and Tower Hamlets, London: Ofsted.

Office for Standards in Education (1999) *National Literacy Strategy – an Evaluation of the First Year,* London: Ofsted.

Office for Standards in Education (2000a) *Teaching of Writing: Could do Better,* London: Ofsted.

Office for Standards in Education (2000b) *National Literacy Strategy – an Evaluation of the Second Year,* London: Ofsted.

Qualifications and Curriculum Authority (QCA) (1998) *Can do Better – Raising Boys' Achievement in English,* London: Department for Education and Employment.

Qualifications and Curriculum Authority (QCA) (1999) *Curriculum Guidance for the Foundation Stage,* QCA/99/436, 10/99, London: Department for Education and Employment.

Peters, R. S. (1969) *Perspectives on Plowden,* London: Routledge and Kegan, Paul.

Pyke, N (1997) 'Heads Condemn Literacy Hour Plan', in News and Update. *Times Educational Supplement* 19 September.

Reyes, M. (1992) 'Challenging venerable assumptions: literacy instruction for linguistically diverse students', *Harvard Educational Review* 62(4): 427–46.

Reynolds, D. (1998) 'Schooling for literacy: a review of research on teacher effectiveness and school effectiveness and its implications for contemporary educational policies', *Educational Review* 50(2): 147–62.

Riley, J. (1996) *The Teaching of Reading,* London: Paul Chapman Publishing.

Sainsbury, M., Schagen, I. and Whetton, C. (1998) *Evaluation of the National Literacy Project Cohort 1, 1996–1998,* Slough: National Foundation for Educational Research.

Sammons, P., Nuttall, D. and Cuttance, P. (1993) 'Differential school effectiveness: results from a reanalysis of the Inner London Education Authority's Junior School Project Data', *British Educational Research Journal* 19(4): 381–405.

Sammons, P., Hillman, J. and Mortimore, P. (1995) *Key Characteristics of Effective Schools: a Review of School Effectiveness Research,* London: Office for Standards in Education.

Scheerens, J. (1992) *Effective Schooling: Research, Theory and Practice,* London: Cassell.

Schön, D. A. (1983) *The Reflective Practitioner: How Professionals Think in Action,* London: Temple Smith.

Sharp, C., Hutchison, D. and Whetton, C. (1994) 'How do season of birth and length of schooling affect children's attainment at key stage one?' *Educational Research* 36(2).

Slavin, R. E. (1996) *Education for All,* Lisse: Swets and Zeitlinger.

Southgate, V., Arnold, H. and Johnson, S. (1981) *Extending Beginning Reading,* London: Heinemann.

Sweetman, J. (1998) 'Gamble on the future' *Times Educational Supplement,* 30 January.

Sylva, K., Hurry, J., Mirelman, H., Burrell, A. and Riley, J. (1999) 'Evaluation of a focused literacy teaching programme in reception and year 1 classes: classroom observations', *British Educational Research Journal* 25(5): 617–36.

Tizard, B., Blatchford, P., Burke, J., Farquhar, C. and Plewis, I. (1988) *Young Children at School in the Inner City,* London: Lawrence Erlbaum Associates

Tharp, R. G. and Gallimore, R. (1988) *Rousing Minds to Life: Teaching, Learning, and Schooling in Social Context,* Cambridge: Cambridge University Press.

Trivizas, E. (1993) *The Three Wolves and the Big Bad Pig,* London: Heinemann.

Vulliamy, G. and Webb, R. (1995) 'The implementation of the National Curriculum in small primary schools', *Educational Review* 47(1): 25–41.

Vygotsky, L. S. (1962) *Thought and Language,* Cambridge, MA: MIT Press.

Vygotsky, L.S. (1978) *Mind in Society: The Development of the Higher Psychological Processes,* Cambridge, MA: MIT Press.

Wells, G. (1987) *The Meaning Makers,* London: Hodder and Stoughton.

Wells, G. (1999) *Dialogic Inquiry: Toward a Sociocultural Practice and Theory of Education,* Cambridge: Cambridge University Press.

Westwood, P., Knight, B.A. and Redden, E. (1997) 'Assessing teachers' beliefs about literacy acquisition: the development of the Teachers' Beliefs about Literacy Questionnaire (TBALQ)', *Journal of Research in Reading* 20(3): 224–35.

Williamson, H. (1962) *Tarka the Otter: His Joyful Water-life and Death in Two Rivers,* London: Penguin.

Willinsky, J. (1990) *The New Literacy: Redefining Reading and Writing in Schools,* London: Routledge.

Wood, D. (1986) 'Aspects of teaching and learning', in M. Richards and P. Light (eds) *Children of Social Worlds,* Cambridge: Polity Press, pp. 191–212.

Woods, P. (1986) *Inside Schools,* London: Routledge and Kegan Paul.

World Bank (1999) *World Bank Education Sector Strategy Report,* Washington, USA: The World Bank Group.

Wragg, E. C. (1998) 'A Mantra does not a lesson make', *Times Educational Supplement,* April 3, p. 20.

Index

assessment of literacy 3, 26, 27–8, 50–6, 71, 81, 84, 146–8

big books 36, 62, 67, 82–3, 89, 90, 96, 128, 136, 146, 153, 167

class novel *see* storytime
classroom assistant *see* teaching assistant
classroom conditions 40, 58–9, 143
classroom management 10, 11, 34, 94–5, 127, 141–2
comprehension 158
contingent teaching 13–14, 19, 98–9,
cross-curricular work 48–9, 84, 87, 102, 162–3, 169–70, 172

enlarged text 36, 42–3, 62, 69, 70, 79, 89, 105; *see* also big books
explicit teaching 10, 11, 13–14, 16, 37, 46, 77, 81, 98, 139, 142, 147, 149, 150, 156, 158, 166-7, 171
extended writing 69, 72–7, 81, 83–4, 91–2, 115, 123, 158–62

Foundation Stage 134, 142; *see* also reception
Four year olds *see* reception

gender 58
genres 43–4, 48
guided reading 42, 63–6, 74, 107, 150
guided work 11, 13, 18, 37, 44, 46. 48, 122, 124, 126, 132, 138, 140, 144, 157, 158, 159, 161, 166-7
guided writing 68–9, 72, 74–6, 79, 90, 108, 131, 147, 150

handwriting 71, 73, 82, 87–8, 147–8
high expectations 8, 15–6, 27, 46, 76–7, 81, 94-5, 106, 111–12, 117, 124, 126, 133, 143–4, 152, 168-9

independence 37–8, 42, 45, 48, 65, 67, 94–5, 99, 102, 119, 123, 147, 150, 158, 169
independent work 13, 71, 73, 82, 87–8, 102, 109, 121, 124, 127, 131–3, 136, 138, 140, 142, 144, 149–50, 159–61, 171
individual needs 66, 101, 116, 125–7, 141, 143, 155, 158–60, 163, 167, 171–2,
interaction 8, 12, 14, 18–19, 79, 93, 99, 106, 110–12, 117, 119, 138, 142, 166–9, 173

language knowledge 39, 46, 48, 96, 158, 168
learning support *see* teaching assistant
literacy hour 35, 46, 79, 97, 136, 161
literacy standards 3–7, 15, 17, 46, 50–1, 103, 118, 157, 159, 161–2, 170

metacognition 13, 91,
metacognitive modelling 27, 36, 67, 69, 84, 95, 98, 115
mixed age classes 20–1, 23, 32, 59-60, 75, 105, 114, 118–133, 134–5, 140–3, 145, 149, 158, 160–1

narrative 41, 63, 74, 93
National Literacy Project 4, 17, 20, 26, 51, 53, 60, 62, 101, 129
National Literacy Strategy 4, 7, 9, 10, 13, 15–18, 33, 38, 48–49, 66–7, 81, 82, 91–2, 120, 130, 134, 145, 164

NLS Framework for Teaching 7, 10, 15–16, 18, 40–1, 43, 49, 75, 81, 84, 94, 98, 102, 105, 107, 114, 122–6, 130, 133, 153, 157, 162–3, 167–8, 171–2
non-fiction 43–4, 102

objectives 7–9, 12, 15–6, 18–9, 27, 38–41, 46, 48, 64, 70, 75–6, 79, 81, 83, 93–4, 105–6, 113–4, 116, 124–6, 132–3, 136, 138, 143, 153, 159, 162, 167–8, 170–1
Ofsted 11, 17, 20–1, 33, 35, 45, 61, 68–9, 100–1, 113, 154

pace 7–8, 12, 16, 18, 27, 45–6, 74–6, 92–4, 99, 106, 108, 114–17, 132, 144, 157–9, 168, 171
phonics 71, 73, 86, 92, 96, 138, 144, 149, 155, 160, 166–7
planning 25, 36–7, 39, 47, 63, 69, 70, 72, 75, 79, 83–4, 86–7, 89, 92, 95, 97, 101–2, 107, 110, 113–16, 119, 121, 123, 124–7, 129–35, 139, 142–3, 145, 154–5, 158, 160–1, 165, 167, 171
plenary 38, 44–5, 64, 70, 102, 110, 122, 128, 138, 161, 167
pupil attitudes 17, 46, 62, 64, 82, 89, 98, 104, 123, 128, 136–7, 146, 150, 153, 157, 161, 167, 170
pupil engagement 13–14, 28–9, 64, 70, 88–9, 103, 106, 110–11, 123, 128–9, 137, 148–9, 164
pupil monitoring 67, 98, 138, 145, 160
punctuation 71, 73, 77, 82, 88, 96–7, 103, 108

questioning 63–4, 90–1, 98, 111, 124, 138, 143–4, 149, 163, 167, 171

reading/writing links 64, 67, 77, 83, 91, 102, 105–6, 116
reception 23, 45, 51–2, 54–5, 121, 123–4, 131, 133–50, 158, 161
research methods 22–3, 27–32
routines 12, 15, 19, 27, 38, 95, 102

scaffolding 12, 13, 48, 68–9, 83, 172
school effectiveness research 7, 8, 10
sentence level 36–7, 40 43, 46, 79, 96, 108–9, 121, 136, 149, 161, 166–7

shared reading 36, 41–4, 62–4, 66, 89–90, 95–6, 105–7, 149, 166–7
shared work 11, 13, 18, 36, 122, 128, 138–9, 143, 147, 152–3, 157, 159, 161–2
shared writing 36, 41, 46, 68–72, 95, 107–8, 115, 147, 149, 166
speaking and listening 12, 16, 84, 90–91, 102, 142, 145, 150, 162, 169–71
special education needs 52, 67, 95, 153
spelling 71, 75–7, 82, 86, 88, 92, 103, 109, 147–8, 158
storytime 66–7, 89–90, 102, 116–17, 155

targets 4, 79, 81, 84, 89, 116, 170–1
teacher attitudes 16, 21, 23–4, 27, 45–6, 76, 79, 82, 87, 92, 98, 102, 115–17, 121–3, 128, 130–1, 135, 152–65
teacher effectiveness research 9, 10, 14, 15, 18, 27, 39, 171
teachers' subject knowledge 10, 43, 112, 116–17, 126, 132–3, 135, 145, 168, 170–1
teaching (pedagogy) 34, 38–9, 41–43, 46–7, 146, 165, 172–3
  change in teaching 4, 9–10, 17–18, 33, 45–8, 76, 81, 91–7, 109, 115–7, 131, 151, 156–7, 161–6 .
  ideas about teaching 10, 15, 44–5, 86, 96–7, 101, 137–9, 156
teaching assistants 64, 76, 82, 95, 127, 139–41, 144, 149–50, 169
texts (quality and range) 42, 62, 67, 86, 94, 98–9, 101, 106, 112, 117, 128–9, 132–3, 152, 157, 160–1, 167
text level 41, 66–7, 74–5, 96, 99, 122, 136, 161, 164, 169
text structure 41
time constraints 35, 83, 92, 97, 130, 145, 152, 154–5, 168

word level 36–7, 44, 46, 75–6, 80, 96, 108–9, 121, 136, 147, 149, 158–9, 161
writing process 77, 79, 83, 101–2, 109, 162